# Major League Baseball IQ: The Ultimate Test of True Fandom

## Tucker Elliot

## 2010 Edition
### (Volume I)

This title is part of the IQ sports trivia book series, which is a trademark of Black Mesa Publishing, LLC.

Cataloging-in-Publication Data is available from the Library of Congress.

ISBN: 9780982675946
First edition, first printing.

Cover photo courtesy of Charles .E. Attard.
www.photogozo.com

Black Mesa Publishing, LLC
Florida
Cover design by Holly Walden Ross.
Black.Mesa.Publishing@gmail.com

Black Mesa

www.blackmesabooks.com

*Major League Baseball IQ*

# CONTENTS

INTRODUCTION 1

FIRST 5

SECOND 17

THIRD 31

FOURTH 43

FIFTH 55

SIXTH 69

SEVENTH 79

EIGHTH 89

NINTH 101

FREE BASEBALL! 113

ABOUT THE AUTHOR 123

ACKNOWLEDGEMENTS 124

REFERENCES 125

ABOUT BLACK MESA 126

*For Dwinner and The Benner*

# INTRODUCTION

**I HAVE A** passion for baseball. I got it from my dad, who taught me to play catch when he'd sneak home from work during his lunch break for half-an-hour or so at least three or four times a week when school was out for summer. My first "team" was the Big Red Machine because my first Spring Training experience led to an encounter with Hall of Fame legend Johnny Bench that I will never forget.

My brothers and I always traded baseball cards at night, spread on the floor in the living room, listening to AM broadcasts of whatever games we could tune in through the static. On Monday nights though we'd trade in the radio for the TV and tune in to Monday Night Baseball.

And when I say tune in, I mean it quite literally.

We had a big antenna off the backside of the house, and a few minutes before game time we'd all take our spots—and I don't mean laying claim to the best spots on the couch. No, we'd be setting up a relay of sorts that went something like this: my older brother in front of the TV shouting *"better"* or *"worse"* or *"stop, right there, perfect!"* … me by the backdoor to relay the message as loudly as possible to my younger brother, who would be outside turning the antenna manually, trying to position it just right, hoping to get a clear picture in time for the game. And of course sometimes the only way to get a clear picture was if a human hand was holding that thing steady at all times. It was times like that when not being the youngest of three brothers came in real handy. On those nights at least two of us would get to enjoy the game.

And then the glorious day finally arrived when our parents paid for a cable TV subscription and our lives were never the same. Oh, we still spent our summers outside and barefoot, playing ball, and getting in and out of trouble … but now our nights of trading baseball cards took on a new dimension thanks to TBS. The Braves became my new "team" soon enough, but more than anything else I became a diehard baseball fan.

And as you well know, trivia is part of being a diehard fan.

Our baseball cards were, of course, our earliest source of trivia questions. As we'd trade it was a matter of habit to challenge each other with the "Did you know?" questions in small print beneath the stats on the back of the cards. It was a matter of pride to be able to answer not only every one of those questions, but to also be able to cite the stats from the cards of our favorite players. We'd spend hours studying the most arcane bits of information.

Life was good already, but then in addition to TBS, one day we came home to find WGN and ESPN. Who knew there was so much to learn about our National Pastime?

I spent the better part of my childhood soaking up as much as possible … and I wouldn't trade those memories for anything.

I'm as passionate about baseball today as I was then. Absolutely love the Braves, and I wish Bobby would change his mind and come back one more year. Geographically my family has picked up another team as well—Tampa Bay—and we're big time fans of Carl Crawford and the Rays, and not just the fair-weather variety, we've been faithfully attending games at The Trop every season since Tampa began play in the A.L.

More than anything though, I'm still a diehard fan of the game, I love everything about it—I've loved playing it, watching it, coaching it, and writing about it, but I've never grown tired of it.

I spent more time researching this new volume of trivia questions than for any book I've previously written—and I hope it challenges and entertains you, but more than anything I hope it stirs your passion for our National Pastime, by far the greatest game in the world.

*Tucker Elliot*
*Tampa, FL*
*August 2010*

*"It isn't that hard to get RBIs when you're hitting home runs—you generally get at least one."*
*— Mike Schmidt*

# FIRST

**THERE'S A REASON** diehard fans get to the ballpark hours before game time. It's not for better parking. It's not for extra time to find our seats. It's not so we'll have time to down an extra hot dog, heavy on the mustard, prior to the first pitch.

It's called BP.

Watching a Major League team take batting practice is without question one of the most exhilarating events a baseball fan can witness firsthand. But we don't go hours early to watch players practice hitting to the opposite field. Oh no, we want to see the long ball, and lots of them. That's why we bring our gloves. It's partly because we want to chase those big flies and try to catch one like we're little kids … and partly because we know if Albert Pujols drills one right at us that having a glove is truly a matter of life or death.

There isn't a fan alive that doesn't love the long ball.

So that's where we begin. Here in the top of the first we've got a heavy dose of big-time sluggers who performed some incredible feats. Let's get going with those two immortal words we love so much: *Play Ball!*

## TOP OF THE FIRST

**QUESTION 1:** The annual Home Run Derby during the All-Star break has been a fan-favorite for a long time. The All-Star break has also been a historical measuring stick for players on a potential record-setting home run pace. If you've got 30 bombs at the break, well, that's pretty special. Who was the first player in history to hit 30 home runs before the All-Star break?
   a)   Dave Kingman
   b)   Willie Mays
   c)   Harmon Killebrew
   d)   Mike Schmidt

**QUESTION 2:** The list of players to hit 30 homers before the break is pretty short, but it's also pretty stout because it's a virtual who's who of home run champions. A few guys have done it more than once, but only one player has made it to the break with 30 homers on four different occasions. Who is that player?
   a)   Ken Griffey, Jr.
   b)   Sammy Sosa
   c)   Mark McGwire
   d)   Alex Rodriguez

**QUESTION 3:** In 1994, for the first time in history, there were three players who hit 30 homers prior to the All-Star break. In 1998, that record was eclipsed as four players went into the break with at least 30 homers. In both seasons—1994 and 1998—there was one slugger who was a part of both of those record-setting groups. Who had at least 30 homers at the All-Star break in both 1994 and 1998?
   a)   Greg Vaughn
   b)   Mark McGwire

c) Ken Griffey, Jr.
d) Sammy Sosa

**QUESTION 4:** Who is the only slugger in history to make it to the All-Star break with at least 30 homers ... for two different teams?
a) Ken Griffey, Jr.
b) Mark McGwire
c) Reggie Jackson
d) Greg Vaughn

**QUESTION 5:** Only five players in history have made it to the All-Star break with at least 35 home runs. The record is 39. Who holds that record?
a) Mark McGwire
b) Luis Gonzalez
c) Ken Griffey, Jr.
d) Barry Bonds

**QUESTION 6:** Who was the first player in history to make it to the All-Star break with at least 30 homers and *not* win his league's home run title?
a) Reggie Jackson
b) Greg Vaughn
c) Willie Mays
d) Dave Kingman

**QUESTION 7:** Frank Thomas—not the Big Hurt, but the original Frank Thomas who debuted for the Pittsburgh Pirates on August 17, 1951, and finished his initial rookie campaign with two home runs—slugged 30 homers in 1953, his first full big league season, and was an All-Star the following year. He later set a Major League record for a particular type of home run—that being the clutch walk-off game-winning variety. Thomas was the first player in big league history to win a game for each of four different franchises via a walk-off home run: the Pirates, Braves, Mets, and Phillies. Over the years several other players have tied his record, most recently a high-profile free agent signee in his first year with his new club in 2010. His game-winning shot came vs. Scot Shields of the LA Angels. Who tied the Major League record by hitting a walk-off blast for his fourth ballclub on May 1, 2010?

a)   Johnny Damon
b)   Alfonso Soriano
c)   Andruw Jones
d)   Troy Glaus

**QUESTION 8:** And staying with that particular home run record ... prior to 2010, it was a member of the Tampa Bay Rays who tied this record by drilling a walk-off blast for his fourth different team. Who tied this record as a member of the Rays?

a)   Vinny Castilla
b)   Jose Canseco
c)   Carlos Pena
d)   Fred McGriff

**QUESTION 9:** On May 1, 2010, a member of the Arizona Diamondbacks doubled and singled in his first two at bats vs. the Cubs to raise his season average to .667. Okay, he was only 9 for 12 on the season ... but, he did start the season *9 for 12*, and even better the player who got off to such a hot start at the plate in 2010 was Dan Haren, who doesn't earn the big paycheck to swing the bat, but rather to make other guys who also earn big paychecks look flat-out stupid trying to make contact with Uncle Charlie. In nearly 40 years of baseball since the DH rule was instituted in the AL only one other pitcher had a better stretch of at bats than Haren's run to begin 2010. A member of the 2001 San Francisco Giants pitching staff had a stretch in which he was 12 for 13. Now that's just ridiculous. Which member of the 2001 Giants pitching staff apparently thought he was Barry Bonds for a spell?

a)   Jason Schmidt
b)   Kirk Rueter
c)   Russ Ortiz
d)   Livan Hernandez

**QUESTION 10:** The Los Angeles Dodgers are steeped in history and tradition, recognized around the world as one of the premiere franchises in professional sports, not just MLB. So to have your name etched in the Dodgers' franchise record book for something no one else has ever done is quite special to say the least. This is the franchise, after all, of Reese, Lasorda, Snider, Koufax, Campanella, Robinson, Drysdale, and ... Don Demeter? Yup, Demeter, who hit only 34 home runs in five seasons for the Dodgers, set a franchise record in 1959 that stood half a century. It was a hot start at the plate that got Demeter's name in the book after he belted five homers with 14 RBI and a .382 batting average during the first nine home games on the Dodgers' schedule that season. No other Dodgers' player had ever posted such gaudy numbers in the three Triple Crown categories during the club's first nine home games ... and no player did so again, not until 2010 that is, when this player batted *.432* with five home runs and 14 RBI during the Dodgers first nine home games. Who set the new standard for hot starts at home for the Dodgers franchise?

a)  Matt Kemp
b)  Manny Ramirez
c)  Andre Ethier
d)  James Loney

## Top of the First Answer Key

___ **Question 1:** B
___ **Question 2:** C
___ **Question 3:** C
___ **Question 4:** B
___ **Question 5:** D
___ **Question 6:** C
___ **Question 7:** A*
___ **Question 8:** C*
___ **Question 9:** D*
___ **Question 10:** C

### Keep a running tally of your correct answers!

Number correct: ___ / 10

Overall correct: ___ / 10

#7 – Royals, Red Sox, Yankees, and Tigers.
#8 – Athletics, Tigers, Red Sox, and Rays.
#9 – He was 15 for 64 on the season: .296, one home run, eight RBI, and only four strikeouts.

## BOTTOM OF THE FIRST

**QUESTION 11:** The National League began play in 1876, thus the player who led the league in home runs that season was, for a brief time, baseball's all-time leading home run hitter. His name was George Hall and he played in Philadelphia. And as the baseball gods often orchestrate, the stars were aligned just so and the result is this obscure yet fascinating bit of trivia: on July 15, 1876, when Hall homered for the final time that season (therefore, setting the first-ever season home run record) on that same day George Bradley, pitching for St. Louis, tossed the first-ever no-hitter in big league history. Bradley won 45 games that season and enjoyed a much longer and more successful career than did Hall, who the following season was homerless and later banned from baseball for fixing games. Still, he was baseball's first home run champ. How many home runs did it take for George Hall to establish the first season home run record in 1876?

    a)  3
    b)  5
    c)  7
    d)  9

**QUESTION 12:** George Hall's home run record lasted three years. Boston's Charley Jones broke it in 1879, and unlike Hall, Jones continued to produce and enjoy big league success, setting another record the following season when he became the first player in history to hit two home runs in the same inning. How many home runs did Charley Jones hit in 1879 to establish a new big league record?

    a)  5
    b)  7
    c)  9
    d)  11

**QUESTION 13:** Harry Stovey tied for the league lead with six home runs in 1880, and then in 1883 the five-time home run champion broke the season record previously set by

Charley Jones when he hit 14 four-baggers. That same season, Cincinnati, in the American Association, established a professional record by belting 35 home runs ... as a team! Well, both the individual and team records didn't last long. That's because in 1884 Chicago and Ned Williamson went on a power binge. Williamson shattered the home run record with *27* (and became the first player to hit three homers in a single game) and his club belted *142 long balls*. The top four home run hitters in the league all played for Chicago! And the reason for this power surge was ...

    a)   Rampant HGH usage

    b)   Corked bats

    c)   Greg Anderson's (Barry Bonds' trainer) great-great-great-grandfather was Chicago's trainer that year

    d)   Lakefront Park dimensions (where Chicago played its home games): 196 feet to right, 252 to right-center, 300 to left-center, and 180 down the left field line

**QUESTION 14:** Ned Williamson's home run record stood for 35 years. Babe Ruth, who led the league with 11 home runs in 1918, blasted 29 home runs in 1919 to establish a new record. The record-breaking blast came in the ninth with his team trailing 1-0. It tied the score, sent the game to extra-innings, and Ruth's club won it in the 13th inning. Against which team did Babe Ruth break the single-season home run record for the first time in his career?

    a)   Boston Red Sox

    b)   New York Yankees

    c)   Detroit Tigers

    d)   St. Louis Browns

**QUESTION 15:** The year Ruth hit 60 home runs, in 1927, he and Lou Gehrig established a Major League record for teammates, combining for 107 home runs. That record fell on September 9, 1961, when Roger Maris homered vs. Cleveland for his 56th long ball of the season—and combined with the 52 Mickey Mantle had at the time, gave the powerful duo 108 on the season. Maris, of course, went on to break Ruth's single-season record when he went yard on October 1—the season's final day—for his 61st home run. Against which team did Maris homer to break Ruth's single-season home run record?

    a)   Boston Red Sox
    b)   Detroit Tigers
    c)   Chicago White Sox
    d)   Cleveland Indians

**QUESTION 16:** A big home run is a definite game-changer—and a pinch-hit home run, well, that's really special. What about a guy who consistently belts pinch-hit home runs? You get a guy like that on your team and good things are bound to happen. Only one player in Major League history has hit as many as four pinch-hit home runs in back-to-back seasons. Who is he?

    a)   George Crowe
    b)   Gates Brown
    c)   Cliff Johnson
    d)   Lenny Harris

**QUESTION 17:** How about the Major League record for most pinch-hit home runs in one season? Joe Cronin holds the A.L. record with five for the 1943 Boston Red Sox, but he was one short of the then Major League record six set by Brooklyn's Johnny Frederick in 1932. Frederick's record stood until 2000. A member of the Dodgers hit seven pinch-hit home runs in 2000 to establish a new record, and the following season, a member of the Pittsburgh Pirates tied the new record when he also hit seven pinch-hit home runs. Can you identify the two players with seven pinch-hit homers in 2000 and 2001?

    a)   Devon White and Gary Matthews
    b)   Todd Hollandsworth and Brian Giles
    c)   Dave Hansen and Craig Wilson
    d)   Jim Leyritz and John Vander Wal

**QUESTION 18:** Staying with the pinch-hitters ... Lenny Harris pinch-hit a N.L. record 804 times during his career

and his 212 hits in that role is also a record. The leader in the
A.L. is Gates Brown, who pinch-hit 414 times. The big
difference? All of Brown's pinch-hit appearances came for
the Detroit Tigers, but Harris … he was a journeyman. For
how many different N.L. teams did Lenny Harris get at least
one pinch-hit?

  a)  6
  b)  7
  c)  8
  d)  9

QUESTION 19: The Major League record for hitting safely
in consecutive pinch-hit at bats during one season is eight.
Dave Philley established this record with Philadelphia in
1958. That record has never been broken, although it has
been equaled. Who besides Dave Philley is the only other
player in baseball history to collect eight consecutive pinch-
hits?

  a)  Lenny Harris
  b)  Rusty Staub
  c)  Randy Bush
  d)  John Vander Wal

QUESTION 20: Gates Brown owns the A.L. record with 16
career pinch-hit homers. Jerry Lynch (Cincinnati and
Pittsburgh) holds the N.L. record with 18 pinch-hit homers.
The player who owns the Major League record isn't all that
close to being the leader in either league, because he
obviously spent time playing in both the N.L. and the A.L.
Who hit a Major League record 20 pinch-hit home runs
during his career?

  a)  Rich Reese
  b)  Ron Northey
  c)  Cliff Johnson
  d)  Rusty Staub

## BOTTOM OF THE FIRST ANSWER KEY

___ **QUESTION 11:** B
___ **QUESTION 12:** C
___ **QUESTION 13:** D*
___ **QUESTION 14:** B
___ **QUESTION 15:** A
___ **QUESTION 16:** A
___ **QUESTION 17:** C
___ **QUESTION 18:** C
___ **QUESTION 19:** B
___ **QUESTION 20:** C

### KEEP A RUNNING TALLY OF YOUR CORRECT ANSWERS!

Number correct:          ___ / 10

Overall correct:          ___ / 20

#13 – Prior to 1884, ground rules mandated balls hit over the left and right field fences were deemed doubles, but in 1884 they were ruled home runs.

*"It helps if the hitter thinks you're a little crazy."*
*— Nolan Ryan*

# SECOND

**WHILE IT IS** true that we absolutely love the long ball, you must admit there's something special about a well-pitched 2-1 ballgame. In fact, there's almost nothing worse than spending an entire day anticipating watching a Yankees vs. Red Sox game, only to have the score be 9-0 in the third inning ... know what I mean?

Offense is definitely fun, but a fast-paced game that is well-pitched and backed up with terrific defense and skillful managing by the skippers in the dugout, well it's hard to beat that combination. So here in the second there are some clutch performers on offense, but we tip our hats primarily to some gutsy pitching performances, some amazing defensive gems, and some exceptional managers who recently guided their teams to the postseason.

### TOP OF THE SECOND

**QUESTION 21:** The Houston Astros began play in 1962 as the Colt .45's, and through 2009, the list of pitching stars to suit up for the Astros franchise is quite long, and very impressive. Only one name on that list, however, can lay claim to this feat—he pitched two no-hitters while wearing an Astros uniform. Can you identify the pitcher who notched a pair of no-hitters for the Astros?

a) Jim Umbricht
b) Mike Scott
c) Nolan Ryan
d) Don Wilson

**QUESTION 22:** Yankee history is long, proud, and steeped in tradition. One of the most magical moments for the men in pinstripes occurred on October 8, 1956, when Don Larsen was perfect in Game 5 of the World Series. Larsen's gem is by far the most memorable no-no in Yankee history—but can you identify the only pitcher to toss two no-hitters while wearing pinstripes?

a) David Cone
b) Dave Righetti
c) Allie Reynolds
d) Monte Pearson

**QUESTION 23:** In the N.L., St. Louis has had its share of big name pitchers—including four Cy Young recipients. Jesse Haines tossed the first no-hitter in franchise history way back in 1924, and through 2009 a total of eight pitchers have tossed a no-no for the Cardinals—one of which pitched a second no-hitter for the Cardinals five years later. Can you identify the pitcher who tossed two no-hitters for the Cardinals?

a) Jose Jimenez
b) Bob Forsch
c) Bob Gibson
d) Paul Dean

**QUESTION 24:** Staying with the no-no theme … Boston's had its fair share of success in that area. Cy Young tossed two no-hitters for the Boston Americans (which became the Red Sox, of course) and one of them was against the New York Highlanders (which became the Yankees). In recent years, Hideo Nomo pitched an Opening Day no-no in 2001, rookie Clay Buchholz tossed a no-no in his second career start in 2007, and budding superstar Jon Lester notched his first career no-hitter in 2008. Not every no-hitter in Boston history, however, has been successful. Just ask this pitcher, who tossed a no-hitter for Boston vs. Cleveland ... but was tagged with the loss in a 2-1 game.

    a)   Matt Young
    b)   Derek Lowe
    c)   Dave Morehead
    d)   Dutch Leonard

**QUESTION 25:** And when you talk about no-hitters you have to talk about Nolan Ryan ... so here's one for you—considering the rich pitching history of the Baltimore Orioles, did you know that Ryan tossed more career no-hitters (7) than every pitcher in Orioles history combined (5 – through 2009)? The Orioles aren't the only team you can say that for either—as 2010 got underway there were four franchises that had *never* had a pitcher toss a no-hitter. Thanks to Ubaldo Jiménez and his incredible performance vs. Atlanta, the Colorado Rockies got off this list on April 17, 2010—and thanks to Matt Garza and his dominating start vs. Detroit on July 26, the Tampa Bay Rays got off this list as well. So ... which of the following are the only two remaining Major League teams to never record a no-hitter?

    a)   San Diego, New York Mets
    b)   Florida, Seattle
    c)   Seattle, New York Mets
    d)   Florida, San Diego

**QUESTION 26:** Only one team in baseball history has ever turned two triple plays in the same game. The Boston Red Sox beat this team 1-0 on July 17, 1990, despite Tom Brunansky grounding into a 5-4-3 triple play in the fourth inning, and Jody Reed grounding into a 5-4-3 triple play in the eighth inning. Scott Erickson was the tough luck loser on the mound while Tom Bolton got the win for the Red Sox.

Which team is the only one in Major League history to record two triple plays in the same game?
- a) Baltimore Orioles
- b) Minnesota Twins
- c) New York Yankees
- d) Texas Rangers

**QUESTION 27:** Orlando Hudson had four hits, five RBI, and was a triple shy of the cycle on September 22, 2002. "It's not my day," he said. "It's the whole team's day. We came out with a victory and we're going back to Toronto happy." Hudson capped the Jays 12-6 victory against this team with a two-run eighth inning home run, and that homer gave the Blue Jays a new franchise record. It was Toronto's 33rd home run vs. this division opponent during 19 regular season contests in which the two teams played each other— the most the Blue Jays had ever hit against one team in a single season. Against which team did the Blue Jays set this home run record?
- a) New York Yankees
- b) Boston Red Sox
- c) Baltimore Orioles
- d) Tampa Bay Rays

**QUESTION 28:** The Topps Company began recognizing its Major League Rookie All-Star Team more than a half-century ago. The list of players to earn recognition from the playing card company is a virtual who's who of Major League stars, but only one player can claim this honor—he was the first member of a Topps Major League Rookie All-Star Team to be inducted into the Baseball Hall of Fame. Can you identify this legend?
- a) Johnny Bench
- b) Willie McCovey
- c) Carlton Fisk
- d) Joe Morgan

**QUESTION 29:** To follow-up on the Topps Rookie All-Stars, as with any awards selection process there is bound to be the occasional player who feels snubbed, rightfully so or not. When the most recent squad was announced shortly after the 2009 postseason there was one very notable rookie nowhere to be found on the list—can you identify the 2009 rookie sensation who was not selected to be part of the Topps Major League Rookie All-Star Team?

    a)   Chris Coghlan
    b)   Tommy Hanson
    c)   JA Happ
    d)   Andrew Bailey

**QUESTION 30:** CC Sabathia's career got off to a great start, and he's pretty much stayed on track. He won 17 games for Cleveland as a 20-year-old rookie in 2001, but was second in Rookie of the Year balloting. He was an All-Star in 2003, 2004, and 2007 when he also won the A.L. Cy Young Award, and then in 2009 he made his fourth trip to the postseason and finally broke through with the Yankees to claim victory in the World Series. Now, for a great, great piece of trivia … in 2007, Sabathia joined Kerry Wood, Pedro Martinez, Dwight Gooden, and Roger Clemens as the only pitchers in the past quarter-century to strike out 1,000 batters before his 27th birthday. And Sabathia's 1,000th strikeout victim was … the same guy who beat out Sabathia for the 2001 Rookie of the Year Award. Who is he?

    a)   Alfonso Soriano
    b)   David Eckstein
    c)   Ichiro Suzuki
    d)   Eric Hinske

## Top of the Second Answer Key

___ **Question 21:** D
___ **Question 22:** C
___ **Question 23:** B
___ **Question 24:** A
___ **Question 25:** A
___ **Question 26:** B
___ **Question 27:** D
___ **Question 28:** B
___ **Question 29:** D*
___ **Question 30:** C

### Keep a running tally of your correct answers!

Number correct:          ___ / 10

Overall correct:          ___ / 30

#29 – Andrew Bailey, who days earlier won A.L. Rookie of the Year honors after saving 26 games for Oakland.

## BOTTOM OF THE SECOND

**QUESTION 31:** On April 5, 2009, Atlanta Braves rookie center fielder Jordan Schafer homered in his first Major League at bat. It came during a 4-1 road victory against the Phillies Brett Myers. Schafer was the fifth Braves' rookie to homer in his big league debut, the first to do so since Jeff Francoeur back in 2005, and the first to do it in his very first plate appearance since Jermaine Dye back in 1996. As it happens, of the other Braves rookies to start their careers by hitting a home run in their big league debut, one of them did so as a pinch-hitter. It was the first time in baseball history that a player homered as a pinch-hitter in his very first big league at bat. And that same player later became the Braves manager. Which Braves rookie began his career with a pinch-hit home run in his first big league at bat and then later became the Braves manager?
   a)   Eddie Mathews
   b)   Chuck Tanner
   c)   Joe Torre
   d)   Bobby Cox

**QUESTION 32:** This A.L. manager is an avid biker, sometimes cruising 100 miles per week—even while his team is on the road! He had his team cruising for real in 2008. Only a year earlier his franchise was the worst in the league, but his players bought into his "9=8" philosophy (nine players acting as one unit leads to one of the eight postseason berths…) and sure enough, come October, his team was only the fifth in major sports history to go from dead last one season to playing for a league championship the next. And for his remarkable achievement he earned the Baseball Writers Association A.L. Manager of the Year Award—missing by one vote a unanimous selection. Who is this successful manager?
   a)   Buck Showalter
   b)   Jim Leyland
   c)   Eric Wedge
   d)   Joe Maddon

QUESTION 33: The N.L. playoff picture shaped up like this in 2009: LA Dodgers vs. St. Louis Cardinals and Philadelphia Phillies vs. Colorado Rockies in the NLDS. The Dodgers and Phillies moved on to the NLCS, with the Phillies capturing back-to-back pennants after winning the series in five games. It took a lot of pieces falling into place for these teams to make it to October, and a lot of credit has to be given to the men tasked with ensuring that they did—which is why one of the 2009 playoff managers won the N.L. Manager of the Year Award. The manager who won may soon be joined by a few of his family members at the big league level—one son was drafted by the Dodgers in 2002, but elected to play college ball at UC Santa Barbara, another son was selected after a stellar career at Pepperdine University in the third-round of the 2006 draft by Texas, and yet another son is now starring at Pepperdine. Quite the baseball family ... so, who was the 2009 N.L. Manager of the Year?

a) Charlie Manuel
b) Jim Tracy
c) Joe Torre
d) Tony LaRussa

QUESTION 34: Staying with the N.L. managers who made the 2009 postseason, one of them belongs to an elite group that has only four other members—all Hall of Famers: Monte Ward, Hughie Jennings, Miller Huggins, and Branch Rickey. A graduate of the School of Law at Florida State University and a member of the bar, he is only the fifth manager in Major League history to also be a lawyer. Who is this lawyer-manager?

a) Charlie Manuel
b) Jim Tracy
c) Joe Torre
d) Tony LaRussa

QUESTION 35: And one more about these successful skippers ... one of them won a Triple Crown in the Midwest

League as a minor league player, and later he played in the big leagues under Billy Martin. Which one?

a) Charlie Manuel
b) Jim Tracy
c) Joe Torre
d) Tony LaRussa

**QUESTION 36:** On July 28, 1964, the Los Angeles Angels beat the New York Yankees 3-1 behind the pitching of Dean Chance—who threw a two-hitter, and would have had a shutout if not for one of those hits leaving Dodger Stadium, courtesy of Mickey Mantle—and the hitting of ... this shortstop. He was 4 for 4, but got some help from Yankee third baseman Clete Boyer, who dropped a foul pop in the first that should have been an easy out. With new life, the Angels' shortstop promptly doubled. He hit a two-run homer in the third, a triple in the sixth, and then with two outs in the home half of the eighth he singled in his final at bat to hit for the cycle. It was the first cycle in franchise history—and the shortstop who did it later came back to manage the Angels for four seasons and one division title. Who was it that performed this fabulous feat?

a) Bill Rigney
b) Gene Mauch
c) Jim Fregosi
d) Doug Rader

**QUESTION 37:** Houston's had its fair share of sluggers—guys who could hit the ball a long, long way. On May 15, 2005, Morgan Ensberg added his name to a very short list of guys who put on a fabulous display of power for the Astros, launching three homers in one game vs. San Francisco. Ensberg was only the seventh player to have a three-homer day for the Astros. Glenn Davis, a powerful first baseman in the 1980s, actually had two three-homer games for Houston. And then there's this guy, who did this fabulous feat not twice, but *three* times. Who had three, three-homer games (*including two in the same season!*) for the Houston Astros?

a) Lance Berkman
b) Jeff Bagwell
c) Ken Caminiti
d) Jimmy Wynn

**QUESTION 38:** A triple play is a pretty fabulous feat. Oakland has turned in seven triple plays in franchise history, most recently in 2000. Would you believe that one player was involved in four of those seven triple plays? In fact, three of them came in a span of seven weeks during 1979, and this same player began all three. Who was the Oakland infielder that began three triple plays during May and June 1979?

a) Dave Revering
b) Mike Edwards
c) Rob Picciolo
d) Wayne Gross

**QUESTION 39:** An *unassisted* triple play is an exceptionally rare fabulous feat. Only once in baseball history has an outfielder turned an unassisted triple play, and that was a player named Walter Carlisle—but he did it in 1911 while playing in the Pacific Coast League. No outfielder has ever turned an unassisted triple play in the Major Leagues—and fewer than 20 are on record, period, for all positions. Even tougher to come by is the unassisted triple play that ends a ball game. In fact, it's only happened *twice*. The Tigers did it to preserve a 1-0 victory vs. Cleveland on May 31, 1927. And most recently, the Phillies did it to beat the Mets 9-7 on August 23, 2009. Jeff Francoeur hit a line drive that was caught, Luis Castillo was doubled off second, and Daniel Murphy was tagged out running from first for the game-ending third out. Speaking afterwards about the play, Phillies manager Charlie Manuel joked, "We picked a good time." As for the player who came up with this fabulous feat, the AP quoted him as saying, "I didn't know how to react. I didn't know what to do. The ninth inning was wild—the whole game it seemed was strange." Do you know which Philly recorded only the second game-ending unassisted triple play in Major League history?

a) Ryan Howard
b) Jimmy Rollins
c) Eric Bruntlett
d) Chase Utley

**QUESTION 40:** On July 3, 1966, Tony Cloninger set two franchise records when he blasted two grand slams and totaled nine RBI for the Atlanta Braves in the same game—a 17-3 thrashing of the San Francisco Giants. What is it about this feat that makes it even more fabulous?

a) He was making his big league debut
b) He had never hit a big league homer before
c) He hit both grand slams in the same inning
d) He also pitched a complete game for the victory

## Bottom of the Second Answer Key

\_\_\_ **Question 31:** B
\_\_\_ **Question 32:** D
\_\_\_ **Question 33:** B
\_\_\_ **Question 34:** D
\_\_\_ **Question 35:** A
\_\_\_ **Question 36:** C
\_\_\_ **Question 37:** B
\_\_\_ **Question 38:** D
\_\_\_ **Question 39:** C
\_\_\_ **Question 40:** D

### Keep a running tally of your correct answers!

Number correct:          \_\_\_ / 10

Overall correct:          \_\_\_ / 40

*"The pitcher has got only a ball. I've got a bat. So the percentage in weapons is in my favor and I let the fellow with the ball do the fretting."*
— *Hank Aaron*

# THIRD

As A FAN of the game, being at the ballpark to witness a piece of history firsthand is an experience you'll never forget. My dad was in Cleveland the day the Indians hit back-to-back-to-back-to-back home runs on July 31, 1963. It was only the second time in history a team had hit four consecutive home runs. Now that's a ticket stub worth keeping.

My older brother was in Tampa the night Wade Boggs homered for his 3,000th career hit—becoming the first, and so far only, player in history to reach that plateau with a long ball. Again, that's a ticket stub worth keeping.

Here in the third we've got guys like Nolan Ryan, who threw seven no-hitters (*imagine witnessing one of those firsthand!*), Bob Gibson, and Gaylord Perry with extraordinary feats on the mound, not to mention Hank Aaron, Honus Wagner, and Roberto Clemente with heroic feats at the plate.

## TOP OF THE THIRD

**QUESTION 41:** You know a lot about Nolan Ryan. Heck, even the most casual fan knows *something* about Nolan Ryan. The man is a legend, after all. The seven no-no's, 5,714 Ks, and oh yeah, his 100mph fastball. So try this one—which uniform was Ryan wearing when he tossed four of his seven no-hitters?
- a)  Mets
- b)  Angels
- c)  Astros
- d)  Rangers

**QUESTION 42:** The first radio broadcast of a Major League baseball game was on August 5, 1921. Nowadays we check scores on our cell phones if we can't get in front of a computer or a TV. It's actually pretty hard to imagine life before ESPN, MLB Network, MLB.com, At Bat 2010 for our iPhones, and the many other ways we have available to experience America's Pastime. And yet there was a time when the newspaper was your only option if you couldn't attend the game in person. Here's a hint for your question: the game was played at Forbes Field. Now the question: which two teams played in the first ever big league game to be broadcast live on the radio?
- a)  Chicago vs. Boston
- b)  New York vs. St. Louis
- c)  Cincinnati vs. Brooklyn
- d)  Pittsburgh vs. Philadelphia

**QUESTION 43:** To follow-up on that last question, the first TV broadcast of a Major League baseball game was on August 26, 1939. Here's a hint for your question: the game was played at Ebbets Field. Now the question: which two teams played in the first ever big league game to be broadcast live on TV?
- a)  Chicago vs. Boston
- b)  New York vs. St. Louis

c)  Cincinnati vs. Brooklyn
d)  Pittsburgh vs. Philadelphia

**QUESTION 44:** Ted Kluszewski smashed 279 home runs during his career, 251 of which came for the Cincinnati Reds. Big Klu's 265th home run came on April 11, 1961, during a 7-2 victory vs. Baltimore. It was significant because it was the first homer in the very first game in history for this franchise ... which after winning its inaugural game, promptly lost eight straight.
a)  Los Angeles Angels
b)  Kansas City Athletics
c)  Washington Senators
d)  Minnesota Twins

**QUESTION 45:** Bob Forsch tossed a pair of no-hitters during his career, but the Cincinnati Reds had no trouble hitting him on August 3, 1989. Tom Browning got an easy win that day for Cincinnati, thanks to an unprecedented outburst by the Reds offense. Jim Clancy started the game but failed to get an out as Cincinnati's first seven batters reached in the home half of the first. Exit Clancy, enter Forsch—who promptly gave up a double and a wild pitch before retiring Browning. What followed next was just ridiculous. Forsch gave up nine straight hits as Cincinnati sent *20 men to the plate*. The Reds set a modern era Major League record by tallying 16 hits in the first inning. After the 14-run outburst, the Reds cruised to victory, 18-2. Here's what's crazy—Forsch was the reliever, yet he ended up getting his name in this franchise's record book for most hits allowed in a game (18) and most hits allowed consecutively (9). He gave up ten earned runs, but hey, he pitched seven innings and didn't walk a single batter. So ... which team did the Cincinnati Reds thrash in record-setting fashion?
a)  St. Louis Cardinals
b)  Houston Astros
c)  Pittsburgh Pirates
d)  Chicago Cubs

**QUESTION 46:** We mentioned George Bradley's no-hitter on July 15, 1876, the first in baseball history. Well, baseball's first perfect game was on June 12, 1880, and it belongs to Lee Richmond, who was pitching for Worcester. And how long did it take before someone else pitched another perfecto? Try five days. On June 17, 1880, Monte Ward pitched a perfect game for Providence. Bradley, Richmond, and Ward never repeated those performances. The first man to toss more than one no-hitter was Larry Corcoran, who pitched three no-hitters for Chicago in a four-year span from 1881-84, and held or shared the Major League record for career no-hitters until this pitcher broke it. Who was the first player in Major League history to notch four career no-hitters?

- a) Cy Young
- b) Bob Feller
- c) Sandy Koufax
- d) Nolan Ryan

**QUESTION 47:** Here's another tidbit on pitching that's very impressive. Bob Gibson dominated the N.L. for the Cardinals in 1968. He completed 28 of 34 starts, was 22-9, and posted a microscopic 1.12 earned run average. For the entire season, how many times was Gibson removed from a game during the middle of an inning because he could not retire the side?

- a) 0
- b) 1
- c) 2
- d) 3

**QUESTION 48:** And speaking of the 1968 Cardinals … how impressive are back-to-back no-hitters? Well, sort of—you see, one was *against* the Cardinals, and the other was immediate payback *for* the Cardinals. Gaylord Perry pitched a no-hitter for the San Francisco Giants vs. St. Louis on September 17, 1968. It was a 1-0 victory at Candlestick Park. On September 18, 1968, the Cardinals beat the Giants 2-0, thanks to this pitcher who came right back with a no-no all his own. Who is he?

a)  Steve Carlton
b)  Larry Jaster
c)  Bob Gibson
d)  Ray Washburn

**QUESTION 49:** Staying with the Cardinals strong pitching, in 1966 one member of the staff led the N.L. with five shutouts. The crazy part? All five of his shutouts came against the same team—the LA Dodgers. Who led the N.L. with five shutouts—all against LA!—in 1966?

a)  Steve Carlton
b)  Larry Jaster
c)  Bob Gibson
d)  Ray Washburn

**QUESTION 50:** The Yankees christened the original Yankee Stadium by winning the first world championship in franchise history in 1923—the same season Yankee Stadium opened. Not a bad way at all to break in a new ballpark. Well, history repeated itself in 2009 when the Bronx Bombers won world championship number 27 to christen the new Yankee Stadium in that same fashion during its inaugural season. Pretty cool. It's also a tribute to the Yankees and both Yankee Stadiums that players from visiting teams consider clutch exploits while visiting the Bronx to be among their most treasured career highlights. And so it was on May 1, 2010, when this visiting player hit two home runs at the new Yankee Stadium, which made him the first player with a multi-homer game in both Yankee Stadiums—new and old—not to mention, this same player once had a multi-homer postseason game at the old Yankee Stadium. Who is this slugger with a unique career highlight to his credit?

a)  Paul Konerko
b)  Kevin Youkilis
c)  Andruw Jones
d)  David Ortiz

## Top of the Third Answer Key

___ **Question 41:** B
___ **Question 42:** D
___ **Question 43:** C
___ **Question 44:** A
___ **Question 45:** B
___ **Question 46:** C
___ **Question 47:** A
___ **Question 48:** D
___ **Question 49:** B
___ **Question 50:** C

### Keep a running tally of your correct answers!

Number correct:          ___ / 10

Overall correct:          ___ / 50

## Bottom of the Third

QUESTION 51: As of 2009, there are only 27 players who belong to the 3,000 Hit Club. It's a pretty elite group—especially when you consider Hall of Famers Joe DiMaggio, Jimmie Foxx, Mickey Mantle, Babe Ruth, and Ted Williams are *not* members. A handful of players finished their careers oh so close to 3,000 hits only to come up short. The closest non-member of the club retired with 2,987 hits. In *Kings of the Diamond*, by Lee Allen and Tom Meany, this player said, "The truth of the matter is I did not even know how many hits I had ... Nowadays, with radio and television announcers spouting records every time a player comes to bat, I would have known about my hits and probably would have stayed to make 3,000 of them." Who is this Hall of Famer that retired 13 hits shy of making the 3,000 Hit Club?
   a)   Frank Robinson
   b)   Al Simmons
   c)   Sam Rice
   d)   Sam Crawford

QUESTION 52: Staying with the 3,000 Hit Club ... who was the first player in Major League history to reach the 3,000 hit plateau? It took him 22 years, but he achieved the milestone in his final big league season.
   a)   Cap Anson
   b)   Honus Wagner
   c)   Nap Lajoie
   d)   Ty Cobb

QUESTION 53: Now here's a real piece of trivia: Honus Wagner is the only member of the 3,000 Hit Club who got his historic hit against a pitcher that won 20 games during the same season. Wagner doubled against Erskine Mayer on June 9, 1914, for his 3,000th career hit—and Mayer went on to win 21 games that season. Also, 1914 was the first time that two players joined the 3,000 Hit Club in the same season. Who followed Wagner into the record book later that season despite batting only .258 for the year?

a) Cap Anson
b) Nap Lajoie
c) Ty Cobb
d) Tris Speaker

QUESTION 54: Hank Aaron joined the 3,000 Hit Club on May 17, 1970, just one month before Willie Mays. Aaron's 3,000th hit came on the road vs. Cincinnati. What was Hank Aaron's 3,000th career hit?
a) Single
b) Double
c) Triple
d) Home Run

QUESTION 55: The 1970s and 1990s were the most prolific decades in terms of players joining the 3,000 Hit Club. In each decade the club added seven new members. In the 1980s, however, there was only one player who joined this elite fraternity of legends. Who was the only player to reach the 3,000 hit plateau during the 1980s?
a) Pete Rose
b) Lou Brock
c) Carl Yastrzemski
d) Rod Carew

QUESTION 56: You know that Roberto Clemente is the only member of the 3,000 Hit Club to reach that plateau in the final at bat of his career—a career, of course, tragically cut short when he was killed in the offseason while attempting to deliver humanitarian aid to Nicaragua. But ... do you know the only member of the 3,000 Hit Club to record his historic hit as a pinch-hitter? Ironically, this same player finished second in the league's batting title race that season—and the players who finished first and third, one spot ahead and one spot behind him, became the next two players to join the 3,000 Hit Club. You really, really gotta love this stuff. Who got his 3,000th hit as a pinch-hitter?
a) Paul Waner
b) Stan Musial

c)  Rod Carew
d)  Dave Winfield

**QUESTION 57:** The Tigers Al Kaline picked up his 3,000th career hit on the road in Baltimore on September 24, 1974—but as it happens, Baltimore was his hometown and both of his parents were in the crowd at Memorial Stadium to witness the historic event firsthand. Kaline became the 12th member of the 3,000 Hit Club, but he was the first player to reach that plateau in the American League in nearly 50 years. Who was the last player prior to Kaline to reach 3,000 career hits while playing in the American League?
a)  Honus Wagner
b)  Ty Cobb
c)  Tris Speaker
d)  Eddie Collins

**QUESTION 58:** This player almost became the first in history to homer for his 3,000th career hit. Closing in on the historic number, he had an incredible game during which he was 5 for 6 with three home runs to get to 2,998 hits. The hits that gained him membership into the 3,000 Hit Club were a more routine infield single and an opposite field line drive single a few days later against Montreal's Steve Rogers—and as for the temporary power surge, he hit a total of seven homers during the season in which he collected hit number 3,000. Who is this member of the 3,000 Hit Club?
a)  Lou Brock
b)  Rod Carew
c)  Pete Rose
d)  Paul Molitor

**QUESTION 59:** There have been some close calls, but only once in history have two players reached the 3,000 Hit Club on consecutive days in the same season. Can you pick out the two members of this exclusive club that captured the attention of the entire sports world by picking up their 3,000th career hits on successive days?

a)  Tris Speaker and Eddie Collins
b)  Lou Brock and Carl Yastrzemski
c)  Robin Yount and George Brett
d)  Tony Gwynn and Wade Boggs

**QUESTION 60:** On July 31, 1963, the Cleveland Indians became just the second team in Major League history to hit four consecutive home runs. The first home run was hit by infielder Woodie Held after there were two outs and nobody on in the home half of the sixth inning. Pitcher Pedro Ramos hit the second of the four home runs, and it was his *second* home run of the game. The player who hit the third of the four home runs was Tito Francona, the father of current Red Sox skipper Terry Francona. And the player who put Cleveland in the record book with the fourth consecutive home run was a shortstop named Larry Brown ... and that dinger was the first of his big league career. What are the odds? Four consecutive home runs, one hit by a pitcher and another a big league first? Want longer odds than that? How about this ... on September 18, 2006, the Los Angeles Dodgers became just the fourth team in history to hit four consecutive home runs, and on April 22, 2007, the Boston Red Sox became the fifth team to join that exclusive club—and in both instances, the guy who hit the second of the four home runs *was the same player!* Boston College professor of mathematics Dr. Nancy Rallis calculated the probability of that happening was 1 in 14.3 million. Who hit the second of four consecutive home runs for both the Dodgers and the Red Sox?
a)  Manny Ramirez
b)  J.D. Drew
c)  Mike Lowell
d)  Shawn Green

## BOTTOM OF THE THIRD ANSWER KEY

\_\_\_ **QUESTION 51:** C
\_\_\_ **QUESTION 52:** A
\_\_\_ **QUESTION 53:** B
\_\_\_ **QUESTION 54:** A
\_\_\_ **QUESTION 55:** D
\_\_\_ **QUESTION 56:** B
\_\_\_ **QUESTION 57:** D
\_\_\_ **QUESTION 58:** C
\_\_\_ **QUESTION 59:** D
\_\_\_ **QUESTION 60:** B

### KEEP A RUNNING TALLY OF YOUR CORRECT ANSWERS!

Number correct:          \_\_\_ / 10

Overall correct:          \_\_\_ / 60

*"Fans don't boo nobodies."*
— *Reggie Jackson*

# FOURTH

**JUNIOR, REGGIE, BONDS,** and Mays—one of them is the answer for our first question here in the fourth, and that's just getting us started. We've got stories about some of the greatest slugging feats the game has ever witnessed, from hitting home runs in eight consecutive games to leading the majors in home runs for six consecutive seasons.

In the bottom of the fourth we switch gears and take a look at team accomplishments—some of them very, very good, others, well, not so much. From slugging records set by the 1927 Yankees to pitching records set by the 2008 Chicago Cubs ... let's see how well you do here in the middle innings.

## TOP OF THE FOURTH

**QUESTION 61:** Fewer than 20 players in Major League history have homered in at least six consecutive games. Only one player has homered in at least six consecutive games on two separate occasions. Do you know which player?

a) Ken Griffey, Jr.
b) Reggie Jackson
c) Barry Bonds
d) Willie Mays

**QUESTION 62:** Of those players with home runs in at least six consecutive games, one of them actually hit ten bombs in a six-game stretch. *Ten!* That's pretty incredible. Do you know which player we're talking about?
a) Jim Thome
b) Reggie Jackson
c) Roger Maris
d) Frank Howard

**QUESTION 63:** And speaking of consecutive games with a home run … the Major League record is eight straight games with a long ball, and it's been done three times. Which of the following players does *not* share the Major League record of eight consecutive games with a home run?
a) Ken Griffey, Jr.
b) Don Mattingly
c) Lou Gehrig
d) Dale Long

**QUESTION 64:** And of those players with home runs in eight consecutive games … who set a record by blasting a total of ten home runs during his eight-game run?
a) Ken Griffey, Jr.
b) Don Mattingly
c) Lou Gehrig
d) Dale Long

**QUESTION 65:** In baseball history, only one player has ever homered seven times in a three-game stretch. Do you know who that player is?
a) Mike Schmidt
b) Manny Ramirez
c) Alex Rodriguez
d) Shawn Green

**QUESTION 66:** One player led the Major Leagues in home runs a record 11 times. That's the entire Major Leagues—not just the A.L. or the N.L., but *both* leagues. Who is this legend?

a) Mike Schmidt
b) Barry Bonds
c) Babe Ruth
d) Hank Greenberg

**QUESTION 67:** This one might be even more impressive— one player actually led the Major Leagues in home runs a record *six consecutive seasons*. Who is this legend?

a) Lou Gehrig
b) Ralph Kiner
c) Duke Snider
d) Willie Mays

**QUESTION 68:** Babe Ruth won an American League record 12 home run titles. The National League record for most home run titles by one player is eight. Who holds this record?

a) Barry Bonds
b) Mike Schmidt
c) Hank Aaron
d) Mel Ott

**QUESTION 69:** There have only been three players in Major League history to record four seasons of 50-plus home runs. Which of the following is *not* one of those players?

a) Babe Ruth
b) Ken Griffey, Jr.
c) Mark McGwire
d) Sammy Sosa

**QUESTION 70:** When Mark McGwire set the single-season home run record with 70 in 1998, he also set an N.L. record with 38 home runs in his home ballpark. When Barry Bonds set the new single-season home run record with 73 in 2001, he also set an N.L. and a Major League record with 36 home runs *on the road* (he hit 37 at home, one short of tying McGwire's home record). The A.L. and Major League record for most home runs in a season at home is 39. Who holds this record?

a) Mark McGwire
b) Babe Ruth
c) Roger Maris
d) Hank Greenberg

## TOP OF THE FOURTH ANSWER KEY

___ **QUESTION 61:** C
___ **QUESTION 62:** D
___ **QUESTION 63:** C
___ **QUESTION 64:** B
___ **QUESTION 65:** D
___ **QUESTION 66:** C
___ **QUESTION 67:** B
___ **QUESTION 68:** B
___ **QUESTION 69:** B
___ **QUESTION 70:** D

### KEEP A RUNNING TALLY OF YOUR CORRECT ANSWERS!

Number correct:          ___ / 10

Overall correct:          ___ / 70

## BOTTOM OF THE FOURTH

**QUESTION 71:** This N.L. team owns a dubious league record. It won 105 regular season games only to be swept in the World Series. No other pennant-winning team in history has been swept in the World Series after winning that many regular season games. Can you pick out this team?
  a)   Atlanta Braves
  b)   St. Louis Cardinals
  c)   Pittsburgh Pirates
  d)   San Francisco Giants

**QUESTION 72:** In baseball's modern era the club with the highest single-season team batting average is the 1930 New York Giants. Freddie Lindstrom batted .379 for the Giants that season, but his average was only second best on the club. That's because Bill Terry hit .401, pacing the Giants to a Major League record .319 season batting average. The closest any team has come to batting .300 since then was an N.L. West club in 2000. The league batting champion hit .372 that season to pace this club, which hit .294 overall as a team.
  a)   San Francisco Giants
  b)   Los Angeles Dodgers
  c)   Arizona Diamondbacks
  d)   Colorado Rockies

**QUESTION 73:** It's probably no surprise that the 1927 Yankees set a Major League record with a .489 team slugging percentage. The Cubs boasted a .481 slugging percentage in 1930, but no team came close to eclipsing the Yankees mark until the Colorado Rockies' .483 team slugging percentage in 2001. The Rockies set an N.L. record that year, but the Yankees still held the Major League mark for two more seasons … until this team posted a record .491 slugging percentage in 2003. This team had three of the top five league leaders in slugging percentage in its lineup, but oddly enough, it had only one player crack the top ten league leaders in home runs—and he only came in seventh.

a) Texas Rangers
b) Boston Red Sox
c) Toronto Blue Jays
d) Chicago White Sox

**QUESTION 74:** And I doubt it'll come as a surprise that the Major League record for most seasons a team has led its league in slugging percentage belongs to the New York Yankees with 32. Can you pick out the National League team that's led the Senior Circuit in slugging a league record 23 times?

a) Los Angeles Dodgers
b) San Francisco Giants
c) Cincinnati Reds
d) Atlanta Braves

**QUESTION 75:** Staying with team records here ... which one of the following scored a Major League record 1,067 runs?

a) 1930 St. Louis Cardinals
b) 1931 New York Yankees
c) 1999 Cleveland Indians
d) 2000 Colorado Rockies

**QUESTION 76:** How about team home runs? Which of the following teams set a Major League record with 264 home runs during a 162-game schedule?

a) 1961 New York Yankees
b) 1966 Atlanta Braves
c) 1997 Seattle Mariners
d) 2000 Houston Astros

**QUESTION 77:** Since the inception of the 162-game schedule, the record for fewest team home runs in a single season is 49. A power outage that extreme is nothing to brag about, for sure ... but it's a record that was set by which of the following clubs?

a) 1963 Houston Colt .45's
b) 1967 Kansas City Athletics

c)   1975 California Angels
d)   1979 Houston Astros

**QUESTION 78:** The record for most runs scored by one team in a single game during baseball's modern era is 30. On August 22, 2007, the Baltimore Orioles led this team 3-0 at home as play moved to the top of the fourth … but the visiting team scored five in the fourth, nine in the sixth, ten in the eighth, and six more in the ninth, and when all was said and done the Orioles lost by a final score of 30-3. The number eight and nine hitters for the visiting team both collected four hits, two home runs, and seven RBI—not combined, I mean they both got four hits, they both hit two homers, and they both drove in seven runs. The number eight hitter scored five runs … but the number nine hitter *only* scored four. Which team set a Major League record after hanging 30 runs on Baltimore at Camden Yards?
a)   New York Yankees
b)   Texas Rangers
c)   Boston Red Sox
d)   Toronto Blue Jays

**QUESTION 79:** The Houston Astros would have loved a little bit of offense vs. the Chicago Cubs during back-to-back games played on September 14 and 15, 2008. The Astros offense was limited to one hit total … for both games. That's a Major League record for fewest hits by one team in consecutive games. The Cubs no-hit the Astros on September 14, and then held Houston hitless until the seventh inning on September 15, winning both games by scores of 5-0 and 6-1. Which two starting pitchers for the Cubs earned the victories?
a)   Ted Lilly and Jason Marquis
b)   Rich Harden and Ryan Dempster
c)   Ted Lilly and Carlos Zambrano
d)   Carlos Zambrano and Ryan Dempster

QUESTION 80: Since baseball's modern era began in 1901, which of the following teams recorded the highest winning percentage for a single season?

    a)   1906 Chicago Cubs
    b)   1954 Cleveland Indians
    c)   1961 New York Yankees
    d)   2001 Seattle Mariners

## BOTTOM OF THE FOURTH ANSWER KEY

\_\_\_ **QUESTION 71:** B*
\_\_\_ **QUESTION 72:** D
\_\_\_ **QUESTION 73:** B
\_\_\_ **QUESTION 74:** B
\_\_\_ **QUESTION 75:** B
\_\_\_ **QUESTION 76:** C
\_\_\_ **QUESTION 77:** D
\_\_\_ **QUESTION 78:** B*
\_\_\_ **QUESTION 79:** C*
\_\_\_ **QUESTION 80:** A*

### KEEP A RUNNING TALLY OF YOUR CORRECT ANSWERS!

Number correct:       \_\_\_ / 10

Overall correct:      \_\_\_ / 80

#71 – vs. Boston, 2004.

#78 – Jarrod Saltalamacchia batted eighth, Ramon Vazquez batted ninth. The Rangers also had two players hit grand slams, Travis Metcalf and Marlon Byrd. It was only the sixth time in history that a team scored nine-plus runs in two different innings of the same game. One last tidbit—the Baltimore Ravens managed to go the entire previous NFL season without allowing 30 points to an opponent ...

#79 – Carlos Zambrano pitched the no-hitter on September 14, striking out ten while walking only one batter. Ted Lilly gave up one hit in seven shutout innings before yielding to the bullpen on September 15.

#80 – 116-36, but lost the World Series to the White Sox. The Cubs then won the World Series in both 1907 and 1908.

*"When it was over, I was so happy I felt like crying."*
*— Don Larsen, on his World Series Perfect Game*

# FIFTH

**IN THE TOP** of the third you read about the first two perfect games in Major League history—Lee Richmond and Monte Ward, just five days apart in 1880. Well, it *only* took another 130 years before there were once again two perfect games in the same season. Dallas Braden (Oakland) and Roy Halladay (Philadelphia) both tossed perfect games in 2010—Braden vs. Tampa on May 9, Halladay vs. Florida on May 29.

We start off the fifth with some perfect game questions inspired by the gems tossed by Braden and Halladay. And then in the bottom of the frame we'll see how closely you've been following the 2010 season as we'll look at some other clutch performers from this year.

## TOP OF THE FIFTH

**QUESTION 81:** Braden's perfecto was only the 19th in Major League history … and Rays' manager Joe Maddon was on hand to witness *three* of them. That's kind of cool. On the downside, he was in the opposing dugout for all three! It was also the second season in a row that his

Rays were no-hit in perfect fashion. Who pitched a perfect game against Tampa Bay on July 23, 2009?

**QUESTION 82:** All three perfect games against teams that Joe Maddon coached for were pitched by lefties. The first was on July 28, 1994, when Maddon was the bullpen coach for the California Angels. Who was the lefty that hurled the gem for Texas that day in a 4-0 victory over the Angels?

**QUESTION 83:** In reference to Braden's game, Maddon said, "I'm a bad omen. That's the third perfect game and fourth no-hitter I've been on the wrong side of ... if you want to see another one, just follow me around." (*No kidding! After making that remark in May, Maddon's Rays were involved in two more no-hitters ... one in June, and again in July—three straight months!*) Braden's perfect game drew attention from others around the league besides Maddon ... including one slugger who earlier had a run-in with Braden. In fact, until his perfect game, it was his altercation with this player that Braden was best known for, telling him to "do laps in the bullpen" if he wanted to run across a mound. Braden was referring to an incident in which the slugger ran across the pitcher's mound when returning to first base after running hard on a ball hit foul. In reply to Braden's remarks, the slugger refused to comment, and then said he didn't want to give Braden an extra "15 minutes of fame." Turns out Braden didn't need any help in that department. The slugger relented after the perfect game, however, saying, "It's always better to be remembered for some of the good things you do on the field, and good for him ... he threw a perfect game." Who is the slugger that Braden squabbled with during the weeks leading up to his perfect game?

**QUESTION 84:** The fact that Braden's perfect game came on Mother's Day took on added significance because his mom died of cancer when he was a senior in high school.

His grandmother, however, was in the stands to witness the perfect game in person. In fact, his grandmother reportedly said, "Stick it—" and then the name of the aforementioned slugger, after Braden recorded the last out. It was a long road to perfection for Braden. He was only a 24th-round draft pick in 2004, played for eight different minor league teams his first five years of pro ball, and took the mound that day with a mediocre 17-23 career record. Now his name is in the record books as the second pitcher in Oakland franchise history to pitch a perfect game. And he etched his name alongside some pretty good company. Who is the Hall of Fame legend that tossed the first perfect game in Oakland history on May 8, 1968?

QUESTION 85: Roy Halladay's road to perfection was a bit more glamorous. He's widely regarded as the best pitcher of his generation, and in fact, on September 27, 1998, Halladay was a 21-year-old call-up making his second big league start when he came within one out of tossing a no-hitter. He settled for his first big league win instead. When Halladay tossed his perfect game against the Marlins, he became only the fifth pitcher in history to own a Cy Young *and* throw a perfect game. David Cone, Catfish Hunter, and Randy Johnson are also in this select group of pitchers, but ... can you name the pitcher who was the first in Major League history to boast a Cy Young and a perfect game?

QUESTION 86: With Halladay's gem the Phillies became just the fifth team in Major League history to claim two perfect games. The first came vs. the Mets on June 21, 1964. Halladay is headed for the Hall of Fame. The pitcher who tossed the Phillies first perfect game is already there. Can you name him?

QUESTION 87: Oakland, the New York Yankees, Philly, and the Chicago White Sox are four of the five teams that can claim two perfect games. Philly is the only National

League team. Can you name the fifth team that boasts two perfect games in franchise history?

**QUESTION 88:** Halladay's perfect game was only the sixth thrown by a visiting pitcher. It was also the sixth perfect game in history to finish with what score?

**QUESTION 89:** The Los Angeles Dodgers have been part of three perfect games in the National League. Unfortunately for Dodger fans, two of them were *against* LA. The first was by Tom Browning and the Cincinnati Reds in 1988, and the second was by Dennis Martinez in 1991. The Dodgers are the only National League team to be involved in three perfect games … but the team Dennis Martinez was pitching for when he hurled his gem has a distinction all its own as well. On July 18, 1999, it became the first (and so far only) team to have a perfect game thrown against it during interleague play. Can you name this team?

**QUESTION 90:** Dallas Braden did something in his perfect game that not even Roy Halladay can claim. Tampa's record entering play on Mother's Day was the best in baseball at 22-8, and that made Braden's perfect game the first in history to be thrown *against* a team with the major's best record. Perfect games *for* a team with the major's best record, well … that's happened three times. One was the first perfect game in baseball's modern era—Cy Young, for the Boston Americans (Red Sox) on May 5, 1904. Another was the perfect game for the Phillies vs. the Mets on June 21, 1964 (so if you know the answer to #86, then you know who pitched this game). The Minnesota Twins were the victim the third time this happened. In fact, that perfecto gave the Twins the dubious distinction of being the first team in history to twice fall victim to a perfect game (of course there are now three teams, including the Rays, in that club). Who pitched the perfect game against Minnesota on May 17,

1998, to become just the third pitcher in history to be perfect for a team with the best record in baseball?

## TOP OF THE FIFTH ANSWER KEY

\_\_\_ **QUESTION 81:** Mark Buehrle, Chicago White Sox
\_\_\_ **QUESTION 82:** Kenny Rogers
\_\_\_ **QUESTION 83:** Alex Rodriguez*
\_\_\_ **QUESTION 84:** Catfish Hunter
\_\_\_ **QUESTION 85:** Sandy Koufax, Los Angeles Dodgers
\_\_\_ **QUESTION 86:** Jim Bunning
\_\_\_ **QUESTION 87:** Cleveland Indians*
\_\_\_ **QUESTION 88:** 1-0
\_\_\_ **QUESTION 89:** Montreal Expos*
\_\_\_ **QUESTION 90:** David Wells, New York Yankees

## KEEP A RUNNING TALLY OF YOUR CORRECT ANSWERS!

Number correct: \_\_\_ / 10

Overall correct: \_\_\_ / 90

#83 – not only did the Rays get no-hit in three consecutive months, but in May, July, and August the Rays were also one-hit by Boston's Jon Lester and three relievers, Cleveland's Fausto Carmona and Tony Sipp, and Toronto's Brandon Morrow, who held Tampa hitless until Evan Longoria singled with two outs in the ninth. Tampa is the first team in MLB history to be no-hit or one-hit a combined five times in one season.

#87 – the Yankees have three, one being Don Larsen's World Series performance.

#89 – vs. David Cone and the New York Yankees.

## BOTTOM OF THE FIFTH

**QUESTION 91:** The Arizona Diamondbacks hit back-to-back-to-back-to-back home runs vs. Milwaukee's Dave Bush on August 11, 2010. Arizona became just the seventh team in history to pull off this remarkable feat, and it was just the third time that four consecutive homers were hit against *one* pitcher. Adam LaRoche, Miguel Montero, and Mark Reynolds hit the first three bombs. Reynolds, who had struck out four consecutive at bats against Bush, said afterwards, "I just wanted to get a hit. I didn't care if it was a homer or a swinging bunt." Statistically, however, the most mindboggling bit of trivia to come out of this night is the name of the shortstop that hit the fourth home run. Who is he?

**QUESTION 92:** The National League entered the 2010 All-Star Game without a victory in the Mid-Summer Classic since 1996. After the 2002 All-Star Fiasco (11 innings, 7-7 tie) MLB thought it might be good to introduce something "exciting" to make the All-Star contest more meaningful … hence home field advantage in the World Series to the victors. And because of *that*, teams winning the A.L. pennant have held home field advantage in every World Series since 2002, the last season it was alternated to the A.L. ballpark. Well, not this year … the N.L. ended its drought with an exciting 3-1 victory, thanks to this All-Star MVP, who hit a bases clearing double in the seventh inning. He later said, "As a kid, this is what you dream about when you play baseball." Although to be honest, as a kid, I always dreamed of winning the World Series … not the All-Star Game. Anyway, you never know, his big hit in the summer could set him up for a bigger hit in the fall. Which member of the Atlanta Braves won MVP honors after leading the N.L. to victory in the 2010 All-Star Game?

**QUESTION 93:** Ivan Rodriguez said, "I've been catching a lot of guys, but this kid is unbelievable." He was referring to Stephen Strasburg, of course, after the

Nationals' rookie phenom defeated Pittsburgh 5-2 to win his big league debut on June 8, 2010. Strasburg became the first player in Major League history to record at least 11 strikeouts in his big league debut without walking a single batter. How many batters did Strasburg fan during his seven innings of work?

QUESTION 94: It took Strasburg only three starts to rack up 32 Ks—no one in history had ever piled up that many strikeouts during his first three career starts. The previous record was 29 strikeouts, set by a member of the 1971 Houston Astros. Strasburg's 30th K, which gave him the record, came on a 92mph *changeup*. When your changeup is in the 90s ... that's really saying something. As for the previous record, can you come up with the name of the Astros' hard-throwing righty who notched 29 strikeouts during his first three big league starts?

QUESTION 95: This from the Elias Sports Bureau: since 1970, only five pitchers have won as many as 17 games and posted an earned run average below 2.00 during their first 25 starts to a season. They are: Vida Blue (1971), Gaylord Perry (1972), Ron Guidry (1978), Dwight Gooden (1985), and Roger Clemens (1997). Well, you can add one more name to that list. After pitching seven shutout innings vs. Cincinnati on August 11, 2010, this Cardinals' pitcher improved to 17-6 with a 1.99 ERA. For all the attention rightfully given to Ubaldo Jiménez and Stephen Strasburg, this pitcher was quietly putting together a Cy Young caliber season. Can you name this St. Louis righty?

QUESTION 96: Stephen Strasburg wasn't the only rookie lighting it up on the field. Marlins' 20-year-old rookie outfielder Mike Stanton, who stands 6' 5" and pushes 240 on the scales, didn't make his big league debut until June 8, 2010, but vs. Cincinnati on August 13 he hit his 13th and 14th homers of the season in only his 53rd game. Stanton also drove in 39 runs with a .571 slugging percentage during his first 53 games in the majors, and when he notched his first career multi-homer game vs. Cincinnati he became the first 20-year-old to blast two homers in a single game since April 13, 2004. As it turns out, the last 20-year-old with a two-homer game also played for the Marlins. He's now with the Detroit Tigers. Can you name this slugger?

**QUESTION 97:** On Friday, August 13, 2010, Nelson Cruz hit his 16th home run of the season for Texas in a Friday the 13th nightmare of a game for the Boston Red Sox. Boston hit five home runs in the game, giving the club 13 homers in its last four games, and scored seven runs in the fourth inning to take a commanding 8-2 lead. For the second game in a row, however, the Red Sox were left devastated with the game's outcome. On the previous day, closer Jonathan Papelbon blew a 5-2 ninth inning lead against Toronto, and the Red Sox lost in walk-off fashion, 6-5. On Friday the 13th, Texas scored two in the fourth, fifth, and seventh innings, and then trailing 9-8 in the eighth, scored yet again to force extra-innings. Up stepped Nelson Cruz, who for the second time this season hit a walk-off home run to give Texas the victory. It also kept the Red Sox reeling. The blast came against veteran Tim Wakefield, who has been pitching since 1992. Wakefield has pitched nearly 600 games, including 150 or so in relief—but it was only the second time in his career that he'd allowed a walk-off home run. You might recall the first time he did that. It was in 2003 ... and do you recall who hit the famous (or infamous...) walk-off blast against Wakefield that season?

**QUESTION 98:** Sticking with young sluggers ... twice in MLB history a player has homered on his 20th birthday. The first time was by a guy named Buddy Lewis, who played third base for the Washington Senators at the time, back in 1936. The second player to do so was Aramis Ramirez, who was playing third base when he did it for the Pittsburgh Pirates in 1998. Four times in MLB history a player has homered on his 21st birthday. The first three need no introductions: Ted Williams (1939), Frank Robinson (1956), and Alex Rodriguez (1996). The fourth player to do so began 2010 by hitting a home run in his first big league at bat. This rookie slugger became the sixth member of the Atlanta Braves to homer in his first big league game, and then on August 9, his 21st birthday, he became the first player in Major League history to hit a home run on both of those occasions—his first big league at bat, and his 21st birthday. Can you name this rookie slugger?

**QUESTION 99:** On August 9, 2010, vs. the Boston Red Sox, future Hall of Fame shortstop Derek Jeter singled for his 2,876th career hit. Already the Yankees' franchise leader for career hits, Jeter's single tied him for the most hits in history for *any player* wearing a New York uniform—that's all teams, Mets, New York Giants, Yankees, Brooklyn Dodgers, any team past or present based in New York. He got three more hits on August 11 to establish a new record entirely. Can you name the Hall of Fame legend that previously held the record of 2,876 hits while playing for the New York Giants?

**QUESTION 100:** And sticking with Jeter and New York legends … on September 11, 2009, Jeter singled vs. Orioles' pitcher Chris Tillman for his 2,722nd career hit, which established a new franchise record for the Yankees. In 2010, Jeter played in his 2,165th game, moving him into second place in franchise history for most games played. In both instances, Jeter surpassed the same legend in the Yankees' record book. Who is the Hall of Famer that previously held the Yankees' record for career hits?

## Bottom of the Fifth Answer Key

\_\_\_ **Question 91:** Stephen Drew*
\_\_\_ **Question 92:** Brian McCann
\_\_\_ **Question 93:** 14
\_\_\_ **Question 94:** J.R. Richard
\_\_\_ **Question 95:** Adam Wainwright
\_\_\_ **Question 96:** Miguel Cabrera
\_\_\_ **Question 97:** Aaron Boone*
\_\_\_ **Question 98:** Jason Heyward*
\_\_\_ **Question 99:** Mel Ott
\_\_\_ **Question 100:** Lou Gehrig*

## Keep a Running Tally of Your Correct Answers!

Number correct:           \_\_\_ / 10

Overall correct:          \_\_\_ / 100

#91 – if you recall question #60, it was Drew's older brother J.D. who was part of a four-homer barrage not once, but twice. That means three of the seven times this has been done in history, one of the Drew brothers was part of it!

#97 – it was the pennant winning blast in the Bronx during Game 7 of the ALCS, NY vs. Boston. Bucky 'bleeping' Dent now has company in the form of Aaron 'bleeping' Boone in the hearts and minds of Red Sox Nation everywhere.

#98 – the Braves beat the Cubs 16-5, the most runs scored by a Braves club on Opening Day since 1900. The previous season the Braves never scored more than 15 in a single game, and scored only 18 runs total during six games vs. Chicago. On Jason Heyward's home run, future Hall of Famer Chipper Jones said, "It was the first of many career highlights for him … I don't know if I've ever heard this stadium that loud."

#100 – Jeter trails only Mickey Mantle for career games
      played with the Yankees. If he stays healthy, Jeter
      will surpass that record in 2011.

*"I swing big, with everything I've got. I
hit big or I miss big. I like to live as
big as I can."*
— *Babe Ruth*

# SIXTH

LOVE THEM OR hate them, you've still got to respect them. *Them*, of course, being the New York Yankees—and its true, after winning the 27th world championship in franchise history in 2009 there were plenty of critics who voiced a sentiment that the title was *bought* through big name free agent acquisitions. It was the same way for the Red Sox in 2004 when people claimed the first title in four generations was tainted because the franchise could outspend the competition.

Well, people are entitled to opinions—it's all good because at the end of the day it's not an accident that the Yankees and Red Sox are two of the *biggest road draws* in professional sports. Just saying. No matter where you are in terms of team allegiance, above all else we're baseball fans—and when you've got a franchise as steeped in history as the Yankees that has to count for something. So here in the sixth we've got a few questions about the 2009 world champion New York Yankees. We've also got some milestone performances from players in 2009 and 2010, and then in the bottom of the frame we've got some great questions about all-time records.

## TOP OF THE SIXTH

**QUESTION 101:** On April 13, 2009, for the very first time in Major League history a pair of teammates connected for their 300th career home runs in the same game. Not only that, but they did so in back-to-back fashion. These stars for the Chicago White Sox led their club to a 10-6 victory vs. Detroit after connecting for their milestone blasts to start the second inning. For both sluggers, it was their second home run of the young season, as they both began 2009 with 298 career homers. Can you name these teammates who reached 300 career home runs in consecutive at bats?

**QUESTION 102:** On April 16, 2009, the New York Yankees opened play at the new Yankee Stadium with a franchise record 11-game home opener winning streak on the line. Unfortunately for the men in pinstripes, the Yanks lost their inaugural game in the new stadium, falling 10-2 to Cliff Lee and the Cleveland Indians. Historic footnotes from that game, however, include CC Sabathia throwing the first official pitch in the new stadium, Johnny Damon getting the first hit (a single off Lee in the bottom of the first), and … the first home run in the new stadium, which was hit by which Yankee veteran?

**QUESTION 103:** Staying with the 2009 Yankees … the club set a Major League record in May and June by fielding flawlessly for 18 consecutive games. No errors for 18 games in a row! Nearly 700 chances handled in that stretch with no mistakes, very impressive. However, at the end of the day, when you think Yankees, you think sluggers—and it was a Yankee slugger who closed out the season with a bang and a new American League record, blasting both a three-run home run *and* a grand slam home run during the sixth inning of the club's October 4 regular season finale vs. Tampa Bay.

Who set a new league record that day with seven RBI during one inning?

**QUESTION 104:** New York added to its own record, of course, by winning the 27th world championship in franchise history, defeating the Phillies in six games during the 2009 World Series. Joe Girardi chose to wear #27 as Yankees' skipper because his goal was to guide the team to its 27th championship—which is pretty cool, if you think about it. Girardi had previously won two world championships as a player with the Yankees, so when he won as a skipper, he joined a very exclusive club, one that only has three members: guys who won a World Series as a player *and* later won a World Series as a manager for the New York Yankees. Girardi was the third member—can you name the first two?

**QUESTION 105:** Bobby Richardson set a World Series record when he drove in six runs vs. Pittsburgh during Game 3 of the 1960 World Series. A member of the 2009 Yankees tied that record during the clinching Game 6 vs. Philly. He also hit three homers in the series, which led to his being named World Series MVP. Who is this slugger?

**QUESTION 106:** The winning pitcher during Game 6 of the 2009 World Series also set a Major League record. He started and got the win in the clinching games for all three rounds of the postseason: the Division Series, the League Championship Series, and the World Series— becoming the first player in history to achieve such a feat. Can you name this veteran pitcher?

**QUESTION 107:** On August 7, 2010, Chipper Jones told this Braves' pitcher, "You're going to have three runs to play with, make it last." And that's exactly what he did in tossing eight scoreless innings to beat the San Francisco Giants 3-0. The win improved his season record to 13-5, but even more impressive is this bit of trivia: during 155 career starts in which his team scored at least three runs while he was still in the game, his record improved to an *astounding 130-2*. Now that's getting the job done. Who is this ace pitcher for the Atlanta Braves?

**QUESTION 108:** On that same date, August 7, 2010, another pitcher posted an impressive performance, and in doing so he achieved a career milestone: 150 wins. CC Sabathia tossed eight innings of six-hit ball for the Yankees, beating the Boston Red Sox 5-2 to earn his 150th career win. Only 30 years and 17 days old at the time, there have been only four players in the past 40 years to win 150 games at a younger age than Sabathia: Vida Blue, Bert Blyleven, Greg Maddux, and Dwight Gooden. Of those four, who reached the 150 win plateau the fastest at the remarkably young age of 28 years and 232 days old?

**QUESTION 109:** And speaking of milestone wins ... just a day earlier, on August 6, 2010, newly acquired Rangers' lefty Cliff Lee gave up just one run over eight innings to beat Oakland 5-1, giving Lee his 100th career victory. Lee's career record improved to 100-57. On the date of Lee's milestone win, there were only five pitchers active in the majors who reached the 100 win plateau with fewer career decisions: Roy Oswalt, Johan Santana, Tim Hudson, Roy Halladay, and Andy Pettitte. Of those five star pitchers, who reached 100 wins the fastest, with only 145 career decisions?

**QUESTION 110:** On August 4, 2010, Derek Jeter paced the Yankees in a 5-1 win vs. Toronto, going 4 for 4 with two doubles and three runs scored. That performance gave him yet another place in Yankees' franchise history. It was the ninth time in his career that Jeter had a perfect day at the plate during a game in which he had at least four plate appearances. Only one Yankee in the past 75 years had as many as eight perfect days with at least four plate appearances—and like Jeter, he was also the

Yankees' captain. Who is this former Yankees' captain with eight perfect days at the plate?

## TOP OF THE SIXTH ANSWER KEY

\_\_\_ **QUESTION 101:** Jermaine Dye and Paul Konerko
\_\_\_ **QUESTION 102:** Jorge Posada
\_\_\_ **QUESTION 103:** Alex Rodriguez
\_\_\_ **QUESTION 104:** Billy Martin and Ralph Houk
\_\_\_ **QUESTION 105:** Hideki Matsui
\_\_\_ **QUESTION 106:** Andy Pettitte
\_\_\_ **QUESTION 107:** Tim Hudson
\_\_\_ **QUESTION 108:** Dwight Gooden
\_\_\_ **QUESTION 109:** Tim Hudson*
\_\_\_ **QUESTION 110:** Thurman Munson

### KEEP A RUNNING TALLY OF YOUR CORRECT ANSWERS!

Number correct:        \_\_\_ / 10

Overall correct:        \_\_\_ / 110

#109 – Tim Hudson (100-45), Roy Oswalt (100-47), Johan Santana (100-47), Roy Halladay (100-50), and Andy Pettitte (100-54).

## BOTTOM OF THE SIXTH

**QUESTION 111:** This veteran and two-time world champion once said, "I was just in the right place at the right time." And he wasn't talking about being part of the Big Red Machine that won back-to-back World Series titles in 1975-76. He's a member of the Cincinnati Reds Hall of Fame—but in baseball circles he's also remembered for this dubious honor, which is what his quote was referencing: he was the 3,000th career strikeout victim for two of baseball's biggest legends, Bob Gibson and Nolan Ryan. Can you name this veteran player?

**QUESTION 112:** Babe Ruth set three Major League records in 1921 that still stand—119 extra-base hits, 177 runs, and this really, really big number for total bases. What is the modern-era record for most total bases in a single season, set by Babe Ruth in 1921?

**QUESTION 113:** Hack Wilson belted 56 home runs for the Cubs in 1930, and that same season he set a Major League record for RBI that still stands. Often overlooked is the fact Wilson stood only 5' 6" ... *in his spikes!* Yet the Hall of Famer struck fear into the hearts of opposing pitchers with his big bat. How many runs did Wilson drive home for the Cubs in 1930 to set the Major League record?

**QUESTION 114:** This one might be trickier. The Major League record for doubles in one season is 67. A member of the Boston Red Sox set it in 1931—and it's worth noting that this same player only hit 155 doubles during his entire career. Who owns the Major League record for doubles in a single season?

**QUESTION 115:** And we'll follow a tricky one with an easy one, just because we're nice that way. Can you name the Hall of Famer who owns the Major League record with a .366 lifetime batting average?

**QUESTION 116:** You know about Joe DiMaggio's 56-game hitting streak. It's probably an untouchable record, and for sure it's a fabulous feat. But how about this, who holds the record for longest hitting streak in the National League … and how many games was it?

**QUESTION 117:** Joe DiMaggio's hitting streak was in 1941, but just eight years later a member of the Boston Red Sox garnered a lot of media attention when he set a franchise record by hitting safely in 34 consecutive games. And while his record was never threatened, it's a good bet that Joltin' Joe was actually pulling for this player … even if he did play for Boston. Which member of the Red Sox hit safely in 34 straight games in 1949?

**QUESTION 118:** Only one franchise in baseball history can boast three different players blasting four homers in one game. As it happens, on May 30, 1894, one of those three players was the first in baseball history to ever post a four-homer game, and all three four-homer games came in different eras—meaning the franchise called a different city home in each instance. Which franchise is the only one with three four-homer games to its credit?

**QUESTION 119:** This future Hall of Fame third baseman made his 15th career Opening Day start for the only team he's ever played with in 2010. Can you name him?

**QUESTION 120:** On August 2, 2010, this slugger hit his 44th career home run against the New York Mets. His blast also made it 16 consecutive seasons with at least one home run against the Mets. He's been known throughout his career as a Met-killer, and the only team he's homered against more often is the Philadelphia Phillies. In baseball history, only two players have had a longer streak against the Mets: both Mike Schmidt and Willie Stargell hit at least one home run against New York for 17 consecutive seasons. Can you name the slugger who's currently known as a Met-killer?

## BOTTOM OF THE SIXTH ANSWER KEY

___ **QUESTION 111:** César Gerónimo
___ **QUESTION 112:** 457
___ **QUESTION 113:** 191
___ **QUESTION 114:** Earl Webb
___ **QUESTION 115:** Ty Cobb
___ **QUESTION 116:** Willie Keeler, 45
___ **QUESTION 117:** Dom DiMaggio
___ **QUESTION 118:** Braves*
___ **QUESTION 119:** Chipper Jones
___ **QUESTION 120:** Chipper Jones

## KEEP A RUNNING TALLY OF YOUR CORRECT ANSWERS!

Number correct:  ___ / 10

Overall correct:  ___ / 120

#118 – Bobby Lowe, Boston, May 30, 1894; Joe Adcock, Milwaukee, July 31, 1954; Bob Horner, Atlanta, July 6, 1986.

*"Don't worry, the fans don't start
booing until July."*
*— Earl Weaver*

# SEVENTH

**AS WE HEAD** into the late innings, we spend some time here in the top of the seventh with some of the games greatest legends. Can you name Mr. Oriole? Do you know the first Rookie of the Year in Astros' history to later win league MVP honors? Can you name the first player inducted into the Hall of Fame wearing a Brewers cap?

That's just a taste of what awaits you here in the top of the seventh. After the stretch we mix it up a bit: first we have some questions about budding young superstars from today's MLB rosters, and then we close out the frame with some questions about more legends. Guys like Ruth, Cobb, and Williams.

*It's stretch time!*

And it's only going to get more difficult in the eighth and ninth …

### TOP OF THE SEVENTH

**QUESTION 121:** Fans in Baltimore often called this legend Hoover, but it had nothing to do with politics and everything to do with his ability to field. Today's younger fans might think Cal Ripken, Jr. is Mr. Oriole, but not so, because that was another nickname for this Hall of Famer who at different stages of his career won MVP honors during the regular season, the All-Star Game, and the World Series. Who is this legend and what is the number retired by the Baltimore Orioles in his honor?

**QUESTION 122:** On August 4, 1985, this Hall of Famer became just the 16th player in baseball history to reach 3,000 career hits. A seven-time batting champion with the Minnesota Twins, he spent his final seven seasons with the California Angels, and it was against his former team, the Twins, that he notched his 3,000th career hit. Who is this legend and what is the number retired by both the Twins and the Angels in his honor?

**QUESTION 123:** He started at first base for the Astros on Opening Day for 15 consecutive seasons. Houston's all-time leader in home runs and RBI, he was also the first player in franchise history to earn Rookie of the Year honors and then later claim league MVP honors. Who is this legend and what is the number retired by the Houston Astros in his honor?

**QUESTION 124:** A two-time league MVP, on September 9, 1992, he became just the 17th player in baseball history to reach 3,000 career hits. On July 25, 1999, he was inducted into the Hall of Fame—and he was the first player in history to be enshrined as a Brewer. No wonder Milwaukee retired his number. Who is this legend and what is the number retired by the Milwaukee Brewers in his honor?

**QUESTION 125:** According to the Atlanta Braves official website this legend is "the greatest home run hitter of all-time." Who is this legend and what is the number retired by the Atlanta Braves in his honor?

QUESTION 126: It was a Cubs legend that made famous these three words: "Let's play two." Can you name the legend who said these words?

QUESTION 127: A four-time world champion with the Yankees during the 1950s, he later took his fiery passion for the game to the managerial ranks. In an October, 1968 edition of *Sporting News* he was quoted as saying: "The day I become a good loser, I'm quitting baseball." Can you name the legendary player and manager who said these words?

QUESTION 128: "Say 'Dodgers' and people know you're talking about baseball. Say 'Braves' and they ask, 'What reservation?' Say 'Reds' and they think of communism. Say 'Padres' and they look around for a priest." Can you name the legendary manager who generally gets credit for that humorous anecdote?

QUESTION 129: The *Washington Post* quoted this legendary Orioles manager as saying: "On my tombstone just write, 'The sorest loser that ever lived.'" Can you name the legendary manager who said these words?

QUESTION 130: Connie Mack, a legend in his own right, said of this man: "There has been only one manager, and his name is…" Well, what's his name?

## TOP OF THE SEVENTH ANSWER KEY

\_\_\_ **QUESTION 121:** Brooks Robinson, #5
\_\_\_ **QUESTION 122:** Rod Carew, #29
\_\_\_ **QUESTION 123:** Jeff Bagwell, #5
\_\_\_ **QUESTION 124:** Robin Yount, #19
\_\_\_ **QUESTION 125:** Hank Aaron, #44
\_\_\_ **QUESTION 126:** Ernie Banks
\_\_\_ **QUESTION 127:** Billy Martin
\_\_\_ **QUESTION 128:** Tommy Lasorda
\_\_\_ **QUESTION 129:** Earl Weaver
\_\_\_ **QUESTION 130:** John McGraw

### KEEP A RUNNING TALLY OF YOUR CORRECT ANSWERS!

Number correct: \_\_\_ / 10

Overall correct: \_\_\_ / 130

## BOTTOM OF THE SEVENTH

**QUESTION 131:** This pitcher earned the Gillette A.L. Rookie of the Month Award after going 7 for 7 in save opportunities, posting a 2-0 record, and pitching 11 scoreless innings during August, 2009. The only rookie to appear in the 2009 All-Star Game, his strong performance during the Dog Days of August contributed to him winning another award—that being league Rookie of the Year. Can you name the rookie closer that posted such an impressive resume during 2009?

**QUESTION 132:** This rookie outfielder banged out 47 hits in August 2009, setting a franchise record for hits in a month and earning the Gillette N.L. Rookie of the Month Award. On winning the award he said, "That stuff is cool to look back on at the end of the year, but we're focused on winning, and I feel blessed that I could have a good month and help this team win." The last rookie in the N.L. to have so many hits in one month was Wally Moon, who got 52 hits for the Cardinals in July 1954. And like his counterpart in the A.L. who bagged top rookie honors for August 2009, this former first-round draft pick went on to claim the league's top rookie honor. Can you name the outfielder that won the N.L. Rookie of the Year Award in 2009?

**QUESTION 133:** The winner of the Gillette N.L. Rookie of the Month Award for June 2009 was a pitcher for the Atlanta Braves. And it's worth mentioning that his big league debut was June 7. All he did was post a 4-0 record with a 2.48 earned run average in five starts—two of which were back-to-back victories vs. the Yankees and Red Sox. Bobby Cox said the award was "well deserved." And to think, his 2.48 earned run average includes the six runs and three homers he gave up during his debut! Can you name this rookie pitcher?

**QUESTION 134:** This rookie catcher made a big splash in the N.L. during 2008. He won Gillette Rookie of the Month honors not once, but *twice*—in April and again in August. The second time around was the most impressive, because as a rookie catcher playing in the Dog Days for the first time it would be easy to wear down. Instead, he batted .355 with three homers and 21 RBI. He also scored 17 runs, and had a monster game vs. Pittsburgh. On August 26, he had two three-run doubles and a solo home run. Add that up and you get seven RBI. No big surprise, he went on to claim N.L. Rookie of the Year honors. Can you name this catcher?

**QUESTION 135:** This third baseman won the A.L. Gillette Rookie of the Month Award for June 2008. He really caught fire beginning June 9, when he banged out four hits vs. the Angels, including two homers and a double. His manager said, "As he gains more confidence … I know he's going to get better." Get better? All he did was bat .300 with eight homers and 19 RBI for the month—and he ended up making the All-Star team and winning the A.L. Rookie of the Year Award. Who is this third baseman?

**QUESTION 136:** George Sisler set a Major League record with 257 hits for the St. Louis Browns in 1920. The Hall of Famer batted .407 with 19 homers and 122 RBI, and his record for hits in a single season stood until 2004—a span of 84 years. Among modern era records (post-1900) that have been broken, Sisler's stood longer than any other. Who was the veteran hitter that broke Sisler's record with 259 hits in 2004?

**QUESTION 137:** Babe Ruth also set a Major League record in 1920—actually more than one. His 54 homers and .847 slugging percentage were both new standards, but he broke his own home run mark with 59 the very next season, and broke it again with 60 in 1927. Ruth came close to setting a new slugging percentage record in 1921 as well, but at .846 he was just short—and so his .847 slugging percentage stood for 81 years, until 2001, making it the second-longest standing record to be broken during baseball's modern era.

Who was the veteran that slugged .863 in 2001 to break the Babe's record?

**QUESTION 138:** Ty Cobb scored 2,246 runs during his Hall of Fame career. He scored 147 runs for Detroit in 1911, a career high, and when he retired after 24 seasons in 1928 he was baseball's all-time leader for runs scored. His record stood for 73 years, the fourth-longest standing record to be broken in baseball's modern era. Who was the veteran that surpassed Ty Cobb in the record books when he scored 70 runs in 2001 to close out the season with 2,248 in his career?

**QUESTION 139:** Babe Ruth actually had three records wrestled away from him in one season—2001. His slugging percentage record had stood the longest at 81 years, but Ruth's 170 walks in 1923 was a Major League record that had stood for 78 years, and after retiring in 1935 with 2,062 career walks, he'd held that record for 66 years. It was Barry Bonds who drew 177 walks to set a new single-season record, while this veteran passed the Babe's *all-time record* when he drew his third walk of the season. Can you name the legendary player who replaced Ruth in the record book during 2001 for career walks?

**QUESTION 140:** Ted Williams batted .406 in 1941, the last player of the 20th century to eclipse the elusive .400 mark in a single season. That same season he set a Major League record when he posted a .553 on-base percentage. That record stood for 61 years, making it the sixth-longest standing record to be broken in baseball's modern era when it was surpassed in 2002. Who was the veteran that posted a Major League record .582 on-base percentage in 2002?

## BOTTOM OF THE SEVENTH ANSWER KEY

\_\_\_ **QUESTION 131:** Andrew Bailey, Oakland Athletics
\_\_\_ **QUESTION 132:** Chris Coghlan, Florida Marlins
\_\_\_ **QUESTION 133:** Tommy Hanson, Atlanta Braves
\_\_\_ **QUESTION 134:** Geovany Soto, Chicago Cubs
\_\_\_ **QUESTION 135:** Evan Longoria, Tampa Bay Rays
\_\_\_ **QUESTION 136:** Ichiro Suzuki, Seattle Mariners
\_\_\_ **QUESTION 137:** Barry Bonds, San Francisco Giants
\_\_\_ **QUESTION 138:** Rickey Henderson, San Diego Padres
\_\_\_ **QUESTION 139:** Rickey Henderson, San Diego Padres
\_\_\_ **QUESTION 140:** Barry Bonds, San Francisco Giants

### KEEP A RUNNING TALLY OF YOUR CORRECT ANSWERS!

Number correct:  \_\_\_ / 10

Overall correct:  \_\_\_ / 140

*"A life is not important except in the impact it has on other lives."*
— *Jackie Robinson*

# EIGHTH

**HERE WE ARE** in the late innings, time to take a look at the scoreboard. How're you holding up? If you want to be among the best when the last out is made then you're going to need at least 150 correct answers—and you've got 60 questions left.

Can you still make it?

Give it your best shot either way!

Here's what you're facing in the eighth ... we start again with more legends and the numbers retired in their honor. Any idea what number is retired for Gene Autry? Or who played in 24 All-Star Games as a Cardinal? Or who the first player was to be enshrined at Cooperstown wearing a Montreal Expos cap?

In the bottom of the frame we look at some home run records, walk-off bombs, guys with power and speed, and some very exclusive clubs.

Don't choke now ... not this late in the game!

## TOP OF THE EIGHTH

**QUESTION 141:** Gene Autry, who gained fame during the first half of the 20th century as The Singing Cowboy, starring in movies and on television, and recording hit records, was also the legendary owner of the Angels for 38 years—from 1961 until his death on October 2, 1998. The Angels won three pennants during his tenure as owner, and though he did not live to see his beloved franchise claim victory in the World Series, his devotion to the franchise was recognized earlier in his life, back in 1982, when the club retired a number in his honor. What number did the Angels retire in honor of owner Gene Autry? If you need a hint, the number was a symbolic gesture much like when NFL fans are referred to as the 12th man or NBA fans are referred to as the sixth man…

**QUESTION 142:** This legend starred in 24 All-Star Games, won three world championships (1942, 1944, and 1946), three MVP Awards (1943, 1946, and 1948), and won seven batting titles. On the Cardinals official website he is referred to as "the greatest player in Cardinals' history … [and] the most popular." Who is this legend and what is the number retired by the St. Louis Cardinals in his honor?

**QUESTION 143:** This Cubs star wore the same number as another Chicago legend—one who made his living draining clutch shots on the hard court for the Bulls—but his 282 homers, nine Gold Gloves, and ten All-Star selections earned him a trip to Cooperstown on his own merits. Who is this legend and what is the number retired by the Chicago Cubs in his honor?

**QUESTION 144:** His Major League debut was perhaps the most famous in all of professional sports history, baseball or otherwise. The Dodgers retired his jersey number on June 4, 1972, but his accomplishments on the field and in life were so great that every Major League team honored his legacy by retiring his number on the 50th anniversary of his big league debut in 1997. Who is this legend and what is the number retired by the Dodgers and all of baseball in his honor?

**QUESTION 145:** A member of Major League Baseball's All-Century Team, he won top rookie honors, twice he won league MVP honors, and he won 12 Gold Gloves, played in 24 All-Star Games, and secured his legacy as one of the most feared sluggers the game has ever known. Who is this legend and what is the number retired by the Giants in his honor?

**QUESTION 146:** Among his career accomplishments he boasts 253 homers, 969 RBI, and he was a six-time All-Star. He was, however, much more than a great hitter. In fact, according to the Cleveland Indians official website he was "a baseball pioneer." And indeed he was. He was the first ballplayer to break baseball's color barrier in the American League. Who is this legend and what is the number retired by the Indians in his honor?

**QUESTION 147:** Inducted into the Hall of Fame in 2004, the Athletics retired his jersey number on August 13, 2005, and for good reason—this reliever saved 51 games in 54 opportunities in 1992, earning both Cy Young and league MVP honors, and capping off a five-year stretch in which he averaged 44 saves and helped the club win four division titles, three pennants, and a world championship. Who is this legend and what is the number retired by the Oakland Athletics in his honor?

**QUESTION 148:** This legend's Hall of Fame plaque reads "power pitcher who transformed Mets from lovable losers into formidable foes." He literally did it all—Rookie of the Year, three-time Cy Young recipient, nine-time All-Star, 300-game winner, and a world champion. Who is this legend and what is the number retired by the New York Mets in his honor?

**QUESTION 149:** A seven-time All-Star, this catcher was the Franchise Player of the Year for the Montreal Expos in

1975, 1977, 1980, and 1984. Inducted into the Baseball Hall of Fame in 2003, he was the first player to enter Cooperstown wearing a Montreal cap. Who is this legend and what is the number retired by the Montreal Expos (and now the Washington Nationals) in his honor?

**QUESTION 150:** His eight batting titles tied a National League record and he ranks among the top 20 in baseball history for career hits. In baseball's modern era players change teams and chase money in the free agent market with increasing regularity, but this legend spent every one of his 20 Hall of Fame seasons with the San Diego Padres, a feat as rare as his hitting ability—fewer than 20 players in history have played 20-plus seasons in a career, and all of them with the same club. Who is this legend and what is the number retired by the San Diego Padres in his honor?

## TOP OF THE EIGHTH ANSWER KEY

___ **QUESTION 141:** 26
___ **QUESTION 142:** Stan Musial, #6
___ **QUESTION 143:** Ryne Sandberg, #23
___ **QUESTION 144:** Jackie Robinson, #42
___ **QUESTION 145:** Willie Mays, #24
___ **QUESTION 146:** Larry Doby, #14
___ **QUESTION 147:** Dennis Eckersley, #43
___ **QUESTION 148:** Tom Seaver, #41
___ **QUESTION 149:** Gary Carter, #8
___ **QUESTION 150:** Tony Gwynn, #19

### KEEP A RUNNING TALLY OF YOUR CORRECT ANSWERS!

Number correct:          ___ / 10

Overall correct:          ___ / 150

## BOTTOM OF THE EIGHTH

**QUESTION 151:** Rickey Henderson led off Game 4 of the 1989 World Series with a home run—a remarkable feat, but the only thing new about it for Henderson was the stage rather than the performance. After all, when it comes to hitting leadoff bombs he's the greatest in the history of the game. Henderson hit a Major League record 81 career leadoff home runs—and he holds the American League record as well, with 73. And for what it's worth, he also hit a leadoff home run for a record nine different teams and by default he owns the record for leadoff homers in the most ballparks. So ... it's easy to see why he's in the Hall of Fame, and that's without even mentioning the stolen bases. In the summer of 2009, however, a current ballplayer made headlines for hitting some leadoff homers as well. In fact, he moved into second place behind Henderson on the all-time list when he hit the 54th of his career. Who is second behind Rickey Henderson for career leadoff home runs?

**QUESTION 152:** To follow-up on the previous question, the man second on the career leadoff home run list behind Rickey Henderson has played in both leagues and for several teams, which means he is second on the career list but he isn't the all-time leader for either league. Henderson holds both the Major League and the American League records. The player who was second on the all-time list until the summer of 2009 spent his entire career with one club in the National League and holds the N.L. record with 54 career leadoff home runs. Can you name him?

**QUESTION 153:** Okay, leadoff homers are impressive, but how about walk-off homers? Yeah, those are special too. The LA Dodgers got a Major League record six walk-off hits from one player in 2009—and four of them left the yard, which tied the record for most walk-off homers in a season. This outfielder won Pepsi's MLB Clutch Performer of the Year Award for his walk-off heroics. Can you name this player?

**QUESTION 154:** Justin Morneau and Joe Mauer carry the big sticks for the Twins these days—no question about that—but when Morneau hit the DL with a stress fracture in his back during the Twins September stretch run in 2009, it was this player who stepped up his game and helped carry Minnesota into the postseason. He batted .325 with eight homers and 24 RBI during Minnesota's final 21 games, numbers that earned him Pepsi's MLB Clutch Performer of the Month Award for September. Twins manager Ron Gardenhire said,"[He] really, really stepped up big time." Can you name this player?

**QUESTION 155:** There were many fans rooting for this Yankee to win league MVP honors in 2009. That didn't happen—but hey, he won the World Series ... *and*, fans on MLB.com did vote him the A.L. recipient of the 2009 Hank Aaron Award, given to the most outstanding offensive performer in the league. Albert Pujols won the N.L. Hank Aaron Award in 2009. Can you name the Yankee that won the award in the A.L.?

**QUESTION 156:** This player stole his 200th career base during a 7-6 victory vs. Atlanta on August 25, 2006. It came during his 929th big league game. Earlier that month he hit his 200th career home run, making him the first player in history to reach 200 homers and 200 steals during his first 1,000 games. The closest any player had come previously was Eric Davis, who took 1,053 games to reach those benchmarks. This player also joined the 30/30 club in 2006 for the fourth time in a span of five years—the first time in history that had ever been done as well. Can you name the player who pulled off these fabulous feats?

**QUESTION 157:** The 30/30 club is certainly impressive, but even more so is the 40/40 club. In 2006, the above-mentioned player did in fact hit 30 homers and steal 30 bases for the fourth time in five seasons, but he actually took it a notch higher and by season's end he became only the fourth player in baseball history to hit 40 homers and steal 40 bases in the same season. Who was the first player in history to join the 40/40 club?

**QUESTION 158:** We've looked at a lot of offensive numbers these past few questions ... so we'll close out the frame with some from the mound. There's nothing more frustrating to a manager than his offense staking his starting pitcher to a big lead, and then the pitcher can't find the strike zone, starts walking guys, let's his pitch count get out of control, can't even make it through the fifth, much less into the late innings. Well, if you're Tony LaRussa, that's not a concern with this righty on the mound, as demonstrated on August 4, 2010, in an 8-4 victory vs. Houston. Albert Pujols hit a three-run homer in the second to cap an early offensive outburst that put the Cardinals in front 7-2, and it was complete cruise control after that. This pitcher tossed seven-plus strong innings, giving up just the two early runs. The win improved his career record to *46-0 during 51 starts* in which his offense staked him to a five-run lead—and he's now won 31 such starts consecutively. Can you name this solid veteran who knows how to pitch with a lead?

**QUESTION 159:** Here's a stat you won't see too often: this pitcher beat the Florida Marlins 6-1 on August 3, 2010, giving up just one run and five hits during seven innings of work on the road. And the emphasis here is *on the road,* because he did two extraordinary things: the one earned run actually *raised* his earned run average against the Marlins to 1.13 during four starts on the season, which at the time was easily the lowest in baseball for any pitcher with four starts against one team; also, it was the *50th consecutive road start* in which this pitcher went *at least six innings*. Read that again if you need to ... this guy is an innings machine. Fifty straight starts on the road with at least six innings ... in today's game, that's extraordinary. To put it into perspective, it's the longest such streak since Walter Johnson had an 82 game stretch come to an end in 1915. Can you name this ace?

**QUESTION 160:** Also on August 3, 2010, Jeff Niemann earned a 6-4 victory vs. the Minnesota Twins for his tenth victory of the season. That made him the fourth Rays' starter on the season to hit double digits in victories, joining David Price, Matt Garza, and James Shields. What's even more remarkable is that all four pitchers are under 30 years of age, and it took only 106 games for all four pitchers to get to ten victories. This has happened only two other times in the past 40 years. Kevin Millwood, Vicente Padilla, Randy Wolf, and Brett Myers all reached double digits in fewer than 106 games for the Phillies in 2003. The other team to do it won the World Series. Can you come up with the world champion club that accomplished this feat?

## BOTTOM OF THE EIGHTH ANSWER KEY

\_\_\_ **QUESTION 151:** Alfonso Soriano
\_\_\_ **QUESTION 152:** Craig Biggio
\_\_\_ **QUESTION 153:** Andre Ethier
\_\_\_ **QUESTION 154:** Michael Cuddyer
\_\_\_ **QUESTION 155:** Derek Jeter
\_\_\_ **QUESTION 156:** Alfonso Soriano
\_\_\_ **QUESTION 157:** Jose Canseco
\_\_\_ **QUESTION 158:** Chris Carpenter
\_\_\_ **QUESTION 159:** Roy Halladay*
\_\_\_ **QUESTION 160:** New York Mets*

### KEEP A RUNNING TALLY OF YOUR CORRECT ANSWERS!

Number correct:        \_\_\_ / 10

Overall correct:        \_\_\_ / 160

#159 – 11 days later, Halladay made his next road start at Citi Field in New York. His line: eight innings, four hits, no runs, no walks, and seven strikeouts. Make that *51 consecutive* road starts with at least six innings on the mound.

#160 – 1986, Dwight Gooden, Ron Darling, Sid Fernandez, and Bob Ojeda.

*"A man has to have goals—for a day, for a lifetime—and that was mine, too have people say, 'There goes Ted Williams, the greatest hitter who ever lived."*
— *Ted Williams*

# NINTH

**HOME RUNS CHAMPIONS** and record setting sluggers, batting champions and members of the 3,000 Hit Club, Little League Baseball and Triple Crown winners, World Series champions and Hall of Fame legends ... this is what's in store for you in the ninth.

We've also got an A-Rod inspired question. The Yankees' slugger blasted three home runs in a win vs. Kansas City on August 14, 2010, so in the bottom of the frame you'll be tested on the topic of career three-homer games. Think you're up for it? Ted Williams is due up here in the ninth as well. You've got 40 questions left to play ... make the most of them!

## TOP OF THE NINTH

**QUESTION 161:** The Phillies originally drafted him as a shortstop in 1971, but it was as a third baseman that he became one of the game's most feared sluggers. He was so prolific hitting the long ball that he posted 11 seasons of 35-plus home runs (at the time of his retirement that was second only to Babe Ruth, who hit 35 or more homers 12 times). He also won a league record eight home run titles. Who is this legend and what is the number retired by the Philadelphia Phillies in his honor?

**QUESTION 162:** To follow-up on the aforementioned Phillies slugger, in 1980 he set a career high and established a Major League record for home runs by a third baseman when he went yard 48 times. His record stood alone until 2004, when it was tied by Adrian Beltre, the Dodgers third baseman. The record fell three years later, in 2007, to another third baseman that was also originally drafted as a shortstop. Who set the new long ball standard for third basemen in 2007 … and how many did he hit?

**QUESTION 163:** A four-time batting champion and 12-time All-Star, he was also the 1966 N.L. MVP and the 1971 World Series MVP for the Pittsburgh Pirates—and he is one of baseball's greatest legends for his exploits both on and off the field of play. To honor his legacy, Major League Baseball gives an award bearing his name "annually to a player who demonstrates the values [he] displayed in his commitment to community and understanding the value of helping others" (MLB.com). Who is this legend and what is the number retired by the Pittsburgh Pirates in his honor?

**QUESTION 164:** It is an honor for any player to have his number retired—but to be honored in such a way by three different teams puts this player in a club all by himself. Who was the first (and so far only) player in baseball history to have a number retired in his honor by three different franchises?

**QUESTION 165:** He was the first player in baseball history to hit a home run for his 3,000th career hit. Okay, so his name might be easy for you—but it might come as a surprise that after five batting titles in Boston and a world championship in New York, it was the Tampa Bay Rays that retired a number to honor his Hall of Fame career. Who is this legend and what is the number retired by the Tampa Bay Rays in his honor?

**QUESTION 166:** Among his notable accomplishments, he was the last Triple Crown winner in the 20th century and he was the first product of Little League Baseball to be elected to the Baseball Hall of Fame. Who is this legend and what is the number retired by the Boston Red Sox in his honor?

**QUESTION 167:** To win league MVP honors is to establish your place among the premiere players in the game. To win league MVP honors *and* lead your team to victory in the World Series—during the same season—can define a player's career. And to win league MVP honors and lead your team to victory in the World Series in *back-to-back* seasons? Well, to understand what that's like, you'd need to sit down with this Hall of Famer from the Big Red Machine and ask him. Who is this legend and what is the number retired by the Cincinnati Reds in his honor?

**QUESTION 168:** His Hall of Fame plaque reads: "A clutch hitter whose profound respect for the game led to universal reverence." Or another way to say it—pitcher's feared him, and for good reason. He batted .390 in 1980, won league MVP honors that same year, and later he led the Royals to victory in the 1985 World Series. Who is this legend and what is the number retired by the Kansas City Royals in his honor?

**QUESTION 169:** He was only the tenth player in history to be elected to the Hall of Fame during his first year of eligibility. On the field, he belted 399 career home runs—all of them for the Detroit Tigers. If he'd hit one more regular season home run in any season other than 1962 or 1966 then he would have finished his career with a true statistical anomaly—that's because every member of baseball's 400-homer club had at least one 30-homer season. And why not 1962 or 1966? Well, that's because he finished both of those seasons with a career high … 29 homers. He came up one short of 30 twice, and one short of 400 for his career—but hey, he did blast two homers during the 1968 World Series on his way to becoming a world champion. Who is this legend and what is the number retired by the Detroit Tigers in his honor?

**QUESTION 170:** He made his big league debut on May 8, 1984, and all he did was pick up four hits. His bigger-than-life stardom only grew from there. He led the Twins to victory in the 1987 World Series, later he hit a walk-off homer to win Game 6 of the 1991 World Series and the Twins went on to defeat the Braves in Game 7 for his second world championship. A first ballot Hall of Famer, the Twins official website says he is "considered by most to be the greatest Twin ever." Who is this legend and what is the number retired by the Minnesota Twins in his honor?

## TOP OF THE NINTH ANSWER KEY

\_\_\_ **QUESTION 161:** Mike Schmidt, #20
\_\_\_ **QUESTION 162:** Alex Rodriguez, 52
\_\_\_ **QUESTION 163:** Roberto Clemente, #21
\_\_\_ **QUESTION 164:** Nolan Ryan*
\_\_\_ **QUESTION 165:** Wade Boggs, #12
\_\_\_ **QUESTION 166:** Carl Yastrzemski, #8
\_\_\_ **QUESTION 167:** Joe Morgan, #8
\_\_\_ **QUESTION 168:** George Brett, #5
\_\_\_ **QUESTION 169:** Al Kaline, #6
\_\_\_ **QUESTION 170:** Kirby Puckett, #34

### KEEP A RUNNING TALLY OF YOUR CORRECT ANSWERS!

Number correct:          \_\_\_ / 10

Overall correct:          \_\_\_ / 170

#164 – Texas Rangers, #34; Houston Astros, #34; California Angels, #30.

## BOTTOM OF THE NINTH

**QUESTION 171:** The defining moment of his career is also one of the most recognized images in baseball history. It came during his days with the Boston Red Sox, on the greatest stage of them all—the 1975 World Series—but he later spent 13 seasons of his Hall of Fame career with the Chicago White Sox. Who is this legend and what is the number retired by the Chicago White Sox in his honor?

**QUESTION 172:** His was the first number in all of baseball history to be retired. Who is this legend and what number is retired in his honor?

**QUESTION 173:** A lot has been made of Ted Williams batting .406 in 1941. The way he played out the doubleheader on the season's final day, refusing to take a seat with his average hovering right around .400, it's one of the many reasons he's a legend. And since we're sure .406 and Ted Williams are a number and a name you could put together rather easily ... well, try this one instead. With a .426 batting average in 1901, this Hall of Famer boasts baseball's longest standing modern-era record. That season he amassed 232 hits, 48 doubles, 14 homers, 125 RBI, and scored 145 runs for the Philadelphia Athletics—in only *131 games*. Who holds the modern-era record for baseball's highest season batting average?

**QUESTION 174:** On August 14, 2010, Alex Rodriguez hit three home runs as New York defeated Kansas City, 8-3. Just days earlier, A-Rod snapped a 47-at bat homerless drought to hit career home run #600. That blast also came against the Royals. A-Rod's three bombs gave him 56 career multi-homer games, and it was the fourth time he's hit three. A handful of guys have hit three or more homers in a game five times: Joe Carter, Carlos Delgado, Dave Kingman, and Mark McGwire. The record is six, shared by two players: Hall of Famer Johnny Mize and ... this player, who won two home run titles, an MVP Award, placed among the league's top ten home run hitters for 11 consecutive seasons, and ranks among the top ten home run hitters in baseball history. Can you name him?

**QUESTION 175:** On July 31, 2010, Dan Uggla hit his 23rd home run of the season to lead the Florida Marlins to a 6-3 victory vs. the San Diego Padres. In only his fifth season, it was the 144th career home run for the Marlins powerful second baseman—a total that established a new franchise record for the long ball. Florida is the only franchise that can boast a second baseman as its all-time home run leader—which just illustrates how remarkable this achievement is for Uggla. The player Uggla surpassed in the Marlins' record book is still active, only he now plays in the American League. Can you name the player who held the Marlins all-time home run record prior to Uggla?

**QUESTION 176:** Ted Williams and Jim Rice are Boston Red Sox legends and Hall of Famers and they accomplished many extraordinary feats and records throughout their legendary careers. One current member of the Boston Red Sox, however, just removed both Williams and Rice from the top of one particular category in the franchise record book … that being career grand slams at Fenway Park. Both Williams and Rice hit seven career slams at Fenway, but on July 30, 2010, during a 6-5 home loss to the Detroit Tigers, this member of the Red Sox belted his eighth career grand slam at Fenway Park to move his own name to the top of the list in that category. Can you name this slugger?

**QUESTION 177:** Babe Ruth, Lou Gehrig, Jimmie Foxx, and Ted Williams are an exclusive group of legends. You can find their names on many records, lists, clubs, etc., but there was one very exclusive group to which only these four names belonged: they were the only four players in history to bat at least .330 with 300 home runs, 1,000 runs, and 1,000 RBI during their first 1,500 career games. Until 2010, that is, because there is now a new member of that group. What current Major League superstar played his 1,500th game in

2010 and reached that milestone with such gaudy career numbers?

**QUESTION 178:** It's hard to imagine a team like Boston doing something in 2010 and having it be a "franchise first," but that's exactly what happened in a 7-3 victory vs. the LA Angels on July 28. For the first time in franchise history all four infielders hit a home run in the same game: Kevin Youkilis (1B), Bill Hall (2B), Marco Scutaro (SS), and Adrian Beltre (3B). The last time a Major League team turned this trick was in the N.L. on April 29, 2006 … and coincidentally enough, one of the four Red Sox infielders who homered in this game in 2010 was also one of the four infielders who pulled off this rare feat during the game in 2006. Which infielder has now done this trick twice and who was he playing for in 2006 when he did it the first time?

**QUESTION 179:** On July 26, 2010, Joe Mauer and the Minnesota Twins beat the Kansas City Royals 19-1. And when I say *Mauer and the Twins*, what I mean literally is on that day Mauer could have beaten the Royals all by himself. The MVP catcher was 5 for 5 at the plate. He doubled, homered, scored three times, and drove in *seven runs*. Just how good of a day is that? Well, in terms of catchers … it was only the third time in baseball history that a catcher got at least five hits and seven RBI in the same game. That's right—only two other catchers have ever had a day at the plate that rivals what Mauer did against Kansas City. And who were they? Walker Cooper was the first. He spent parts of 18 seasons in the majors and put together a nice career playing for several different teams. His big game, however, came as a member of the Cincinnati Reds on July 6, 1949, when he pummeled the Chicago Cubs with *six hits and ten RBI*. The other catcher is a more familiar name. On July 16, 2004, he banged out five hits and seven RBI as his Cleveland Indians destroyed the Seattle Mariners, 18-6. Can you name him?

**QUESTION 180:** In 2010, as Yankees fans were on "watch" for A-Rod's 600th career home run, one of A-Rod's teammates actually reached a significant milestone of his own: 1,000 career hits. True, at the time there was nearly 100 other active players with as many hits, however ... only six active players reached 1,000 hits faster: Ichiro Suzuki, Todd Helton, Albert Pujols, Derek Jeter, Vladimir Guerrero, and Matt Holliday. Which member of the New York Yankees collected his 1,000th career hit in 2010 at a faster rate than all but six of his peers?

## BOTTOM OF THE NINTH ANSWER KEY

\_\_\_ **QUESTION 171:** Carlton Fisk, #72
\_\_\_ **QUESTION 172:** Lou Gehrig, #4
\_\_\_ **QUESTION 173:** Nap Lajoie
\_\_\_ **QUESTION 174:** Sammy Sosa
\_\_\_ **QUESTION 175:** Mike Lowell
\_\_\_ **QUESTION 176:** David Ortiz
\_\_\_ **QUESTION 177:** Albert Pujols*
\_\_\_ **QUESTION 178:** Bill Hall, Milwaukee Brewers*
\_\_\_ **QUESTION 179:** Victor Martinez
\_\_\_ **QUESTION 180:** Robinson Cano

### KEEP A RUNNING TALLY OF YOUR CORRECT ANSWERS!

Number correct:          \_\_\_ / 10

Overall correct:          \_\_\_ / 180

#177 – the Cardinals' slugger was 0 for 4 in the game, but his career numbers at the time were insane: .331 average, 389 home runs, 1,132 runs, and 1,183 RBI.

#178 – along with Prince Fielder, Rickie Weeks, and J.J. Hardy.

*"I don't want to be Babe Ruth. He was a great ballplayer. I'm not trying to replace him. The record is there and I want to break it, but that isn't replacing Babe Ruth."*
— Roger Maris

# FREE BASEBALL!

**SKIP CARAY WAS** my favorite announcer as I grew up listening to the Braves on TBS and on the radio. One night, listening to a game that was headed into extra-innings, the broadcast was just breaking away to commercial when Skip said, "Free baseball in Atlanta!"

One of the best lines I've ever heard.

I loved it! And ever since I've always referred to extra-innings as free baseball. I was at Game 3 of the Division Series between Atlanta and Colorado on October 6, 1995, when it moved into extra-innings. My brother was in the stands with me and I turned, slapped him a high-five because the Braves had tied it in the bottom of the ninth, and then shouted in my best (yet still really bad) Skip Caray imitation, "Free baseball in Atlanta!"

I swear a roar went up from the section all around us as others heard what I'd yelled. I wasn't the only one there who grew up listening to Skip and Pete.

Well, here we are in the final chapter ... the tenth inning, free baseball. The questions coming up range

from all-time records set by Babe Ruth, Roger Maris, and
Hank Aaron, to guys like Frank Robinson, Alex
Rodriguez, and Cal Ripken, Jr. You've got 20 questions
left ... but they're not going to be easy. Leave it all out
on the field, as they say.

## TOP OF THE TENTH

**QUESTION 181:** How many times did Babe Ruth set the
single-season home run record?

**QUESTION 182:** Roger Maris set the single-season home run
record on October 1, 1961. Who was born exactly two years
later on October 1, 1963?

**QUESTION 183:** Who hit more home runs for his second
ball club—Babe Ruth (New York Yankees) or Barry Bonds
(San Francisco Giants)?

**QUESTION 184:** Carlton Fisk is a legendary figure for two
franchises—the Chicago White sox and the Boston Red Sox.
His most notable home run obviously came in the
postseason for Boston, but ... for which team did he blast
the majority of his A.L. record 351 home runs as a catcher?

**QUESTION 185:** You read earlier that Rickey Henderson hit
at least one leadoff home run for a Major League record nine
different franchises—for which team did he hit the most
leadoff home runs, the Oakland Athletics or New York
Yankees?

**QUESTION 186:** You obviously know that Hank Aaron hit
more career home runs than did his brother Tommie (755 to
13, not even close, or even fair for that matter). But who hit
the most career home runs among the Ferrell brothers? Rick
is a Hall of Fame catcher who hit .281 during 18 seasons
with the St. Louis Browns, Boston Red Sox, and Washington
Senators. Wes isn't in the Hall of Fame, but he was a six-
time 20-game winner who pitched for the Cleveland Indians,

Boston Red Sox, Washington Senators, New York Yankees, Brooklyn Dodgers, and Boston Braves. Wes also owns the Major League record for most career home runs as a pitcher—and he added one more bomb while playing 13 games in the outfield. So ... who hit more home runs, Rick or Wes Ferrell, the Hall of Fame catcher or the All-Star pitcher?

**QUESTION 187:** Instead of brother vs. brother, how about righty vs. righty? Who holds the A.L. record for most career home runs by a right-handed batter—Frank Robinson, Alex Rodriguez, or Harmon Killebrew?

**QUESTION 188:** Or ... shortstop vs. shortstop. Who holds the Major League record for most career home runs by a shortstop—Ernie Banks or Cal Ripken, Jr.?

**QUESTION 189:** Even better, how about clutch home runs ... who holds the Major League record with 22 extra-inning home runs—Babe Ruth or Willie Mays?

**QUESTION 190:** Nothing like starting the season with a bang! The record for home runs during an Opening Day game is three—shared by George Bell (Blue Jays), Tuffy Rhodes (Cubs), and Dmitri Young (Tigers). In terms of *career* Opening Day homers, the record is eight—and two players share it. Which pair of players holds this spectacular record—Eddie Mathews and Willie Mays, or Ken Griffey, Jr. and Frank Robinson?

## TOP OF THE TENTH ANSWER KEY

___ **QUESTION 181:** 4
___ **QUESTION 182:** Mark McGwire
___ **QUESTION 183:** Ruth, 659; Bonds, 586
___ **QUESTION 184:** Chicago, 194; Boston, 157
___ **QUESTION 185:** Oakland, 43; New York, 24
___ **QUESTION 186:** Wes, 38; Rick, 28
___ **QUESTION 187:** Alex Rodriguez
___ **QUESTION 188:** Cal Ripken, Jr.
___ **QUESTION 189:** Willie Mays
___ **QUESTION 190:** Griffey, Jr. and Robinson

### KEEP A RUNNING TALLY OF YOUR CORRECT ANSWERS!

Number correct:         ___ / 10

Overall correct:         ___ / 190

#181 – Including three consecutive seasons.

#182 – 35 years later, exactly two days before what would have been Roger Maris' 64th birthday, McGwire became the first player in history to hit 62 home runs in a season.

## BOTTOM OF THE TENTH

**QUESTION 191:** Guys who hit the ball a long way draw big crowds, even on the road. Hey, don't we all wish just for one day we could have a BP session even half as powerful as what Albert Pujols does on a daily basis? Of course we do. That's why so many people have seen these guys take pregame BP: Barry Bonds and Sammy Sosa. They were always a huge draw when playing the role of visitor—but of these two, which one actually owns the Major League record for hitting a home run in the most ballparks?

**QUESTION 192:** Ever wondered what it felt like to stand up at the plate with Roger Clemens on the mound? In his prime? Well, it didn't bother this rookie because he took Rocket out of the yard for his first career home run. Now he's a member of the 600 Home Run Club. Who is this player—Ken Griffey, Jr. or Sammy Sosa?

**QUESTION 193:** Two brothers who both made it to the big leagues became crucial players in two of the most memorable home runs in baseball history—one as a pitcher, the other as a hitter. The older brother gave up Hank Aaron's 700th career home run on July 21, 1973. The younger brother, ten years and three days later, hit a dramatic game-changing home run at Yankee Stadium against future-Hall of Famer Goose Gossage on July 24, 1983—a moment that will forever be remembered as the Pine Tar Home Run. What are the names of these two brothers?

**QUESTION 194:** The New York Yankees led two games to one in the best-of-seven 1964 World Series vs. the St. Louis Cardinals, and held a 3-0 lead in the sixth inning of Game 4 with Al Downing going strong on the mound. Then everything fell apart. A couple of singles before a harmless fly out, but then an E4 loaded the bases instead of letting the Yankees escape with an inning-ending DP. Ken Boyer made the Yankees pay, and his grand slam that provided the 4-3 margin of victory is one of the biggest hits in postseason history. Instead of trailing three games to one, the series was even, and the Cardinals went on to claim victory in a tough seven-game series. Now, if you're Al Downing, how do you get baseball fans to forget that you were a World Series goat? Uh, well, it's actually pretty easy so long as you're patient. That's because ten years later it was Downing on the mound who gave up an even more historic home run—and this one, people will never forget. What historic home run did Downing give up ten years after the World Series grand slam debacle?

**QUESTION 195:** The most successful any offensive player can be is to claim the Triple Crown. There was a 45-year gap between Carl Yastrzemski and Miguel Cabrera, and there were only 14 total in the 20th century—since the advent of baseball's modern era. You already know that Carl Yastrzemski won the 1967 Triple Crown, which makes him the answer to one of the most popular baseball trivia questions around, so try this one instead: which team has had the most Triple Crown winners in A.L. history—the Boston Red Sox or the New York Yankees?

**QUESTION 196:** Ted Williams won two Triple Crowns, but he did not earn that distinction when he batted .406 in 1941. He won the batting title, obviously, and he also led the league with 37 home runs, but he trailed Joe DiMaggio in RBI, 125 to 120 (and DiMaggio won league MVP honors, having also hit in 56 consecutive games that season). There has only been one A.L. player to bat .400 during a Triple Crown season, and that was Nap Lajoie, who hit .422 in 1901. In baseball's modern era, there have been two instances of a Triple Crown winner in the N.L. batting .400—and it was the same guy both times. Who hit .401 and .403 on his way to winning two Triple Crowns in the N.L.— Chuck Klein or Rogers Hornsby?

**QUESTION 197:** Paul Hines, playing for Providence in 1878, was baseball's first Triple Crown winner. His numbers: .358, four homers, and 50 RBI. The RBI total is hard to verify because it wasn't an official stat until 1920. Home runs are always skewed too because of the dead ball era and the dimensions of the parks in which games were played—but having said all of that, in baseball's modern era the lowest home run total for a Triple Crown winner is nine. Who won the Triple Crown despite hitting only nine home runs—Heinie Zimmerman or Ty Cobb?

**QUESTION 198:** Here's some insane numbers for you—Hall of Fame pitcher Al Spalding was 252-65 during his career … and he played only *seven seasons*. It took him only five seasons to reach 200 career wins—and from the inception of the N.L. in 1876, Spalding was baseball's first career leader for wins. And what's crazier still, he really only played *six seasons*. Spalding was only 26-years old in his final season, 1877, and he made just four appearances with a 1-0 record. And in case you're curious about the name Spalding, you got it—same guy, he and his brother established Spalding sporting goods stores all over the country. Cy Young became baseball's all-time leader for wins in 1903—and with 511 to his name, he'll never be caught. Spalding and Young are two members in a group that is among the most elite in all of sports, not just baseball. Seriously, can you name anyone else who has ever topped baseball's career list for wins? If you can, that's impressive. If you can't, don't feel bad because you're not alone—and luckily, to get this question right you don't need the names, you just need to answer this: how many different pitchers have topped the list as baseball's all-time leader for wins?

**QUESTION 199:** There are some stat clubs ballplayers would rather avoid membership into if at all possible—say, those who have fanned at the plate 200-plus times in a single season (and that list really seems to be growing lately…), or pitchers who have lost 20 games in a season. And then there are those elite clubs, such as 300 wins or 3,000 strikeouts—those are the ones we want. In recent years we've seen some big names reach these milestones—both the 300 win and 3,000 strikeout plateaus. Surely you've noticed, haven't you?

So tell us, who gained membership into the 3,000 Strikeout Club the fastest by date—Greg Maddux or Curt Schilling?

**QUESTION 200:** You've reached the end. Sounds like an appropriate time to include a question about closers ... so here we go: only two pitchers in history have recorded 500 saves—Trevor Hoffman and Mariano Rivera. And Hoffman began 2010 just nine saves shy of 600. Hoffman and Rivera share a career high of 53 saves in a single season. Rivera has actually hit 50 saves in a season twice, something Hoffman never managed to do. Now ... Hoffman or Rivera—who has led his respective league in saves the most number of times?

## BOTTOM OF THE TENTH ANSWER KEY

___ **QUESTION 191:** Sammy Sosa, 45; Barry Bonds, 36
___ **QUESTION 192:** Sammy Sosa
___ **QUESTION 193:** Ken Brett, George Brett
___ **QUESTION 194:** Hank Aaron, #715
___ **QUESTION 195:** Boston, 3; New York 2
___ **QUESTION 196:** Rogers Hornsby
___ **QUESTION 197:** Ty Cobb
___ **QUESTION 198:** 4
___ **QUESTION 199:** Greg Maddux, 2005; Curt Schilling, 2006
___ **QUESTION 200:** Rivera, 3; Hoffman 2

### KEEP A RUNNING TALLY OF YOUR CORRECT ANSWERS!

Number correct:          ___ / 10

Overall correct:          ___ / 200

#198 – Spalding, Bobby Mathews, Pud Galvin, and Young.

# MAJOR LEAGUE BASEBALL IQ

**IT'S TIME TO** find out your MLB IQ. Add your total from all ten chapters and see how you did! Here's how it breaks down:

| | |
|---|---|
| GENIUS MLB IQ EXCEEDS ROY HOBBS, BABE RUTH, & ALBERT PUJOLS | = 190-200 |
| GENIUS MLB IQ DESTINED TO BE A FIRST BALLOT HALL OF FAMER | = 180-189 |
| GENIUS MLB IQ IS WORTHY OF A WORLD CHAMPIONSHIP | = 170-179 |
| SUPERIOR MLB IQ IS WORTHY OF LEGENDARY STATUS | = 160-169 |
| SUPERIOR MLB IQ MAKES YOU ONE OF THE ALL-TIME GREATS | = 150-159 |
| OUTSTANDING MLB IQ THAT PLACES YOU AMONG THE TOP PLAYERS | = 140-149 |
| ABOVE AVERAGE MLB IQ THAT EARNS YOU A NICE PAYCHECK | = 130-139 |
| SOLID MLB IQ THAT LETS YOU PLAY BALL FOR A LIVING | = 120-129 |
| AVERAGE MLB IQ GOOD ENOUGH TO GET YOU TO THE SHOW | = 110-119 |
| AVERAGE MLB IQ GOT YOU A CUP OF COFFEE BUT THAT'S ALL | = 100-109 |

How'd you do? I'd like to know. Send me an email: tckrelliot@gmail.com

Be sure to tell me how many questions you got right, and if you scored high enough, you might just make your way onto a Hall of Fame list to be included in Volume II of MLB IQ.

If you enjoyed reading this book, please consider posting a review online at Amazon.com or wherever you buy books— and don't be shy about posting your MLB IQ there either!

# ABOUT THE AUTHOR

**TUCKER ELLIOT IS** a Georgia native and a diehard Braves fan. A former high school athletic director and varsity baseball coach, he now resides and writes full time in Tampa, FL.

# ACKNOWLEDGEMENTS

**IF YOU LOVE** baseball and trivia then surely you love fantasy baseball as well. My fantasy league this year, RMS 2010, has been outstanding.

I began writing this book about the same time we began forming our league, and the camaraderie, competitive spirit, and extraordinarily high level of "smack talk" produced by RMS 2010 has not only kept me laughing, but it's forced me to work harder to win while simultaneously allowing me to also enjoy this season more than any in recent memory. There are several questions in this book that were inspired by conversations and debates I had with you guys, so special thanks to my fellow competitors: Santee Jackson, Taylor Simpson, Kevin Parvizi, Lorenzo Rodriguez, Tommy Massa, Kameron Allen, Joe Mazzara, Sam Friday, and Connor Novotny. Oh, and Connor, sorry for listing the names by order of the standings … better luck in football season.

# REFERENCES

**WEBSITES**
Baseball-reference.com
MLB.com (and the official team sites through MLB.com)
BaseballHallofFame.org
ESPN.com

**BOOKS**
*Baseball, an Illustrated History*, Geoffrey C. Ward and Ken
          Burns
*The Team by Team Encyclopedia of Major League Baseball*, Dennis
          Purdy
*The Unofficial Guide to Baseball's Most Unusual Records*, Bob
          Mackin
*The 2005 ESPN Baseball Encyclopedia*, edited by Pete Palmer
          and Gary Gillette
*100 Years of the World Series*, Eric Enders

# ABOUT BLACK MESA

Look for these other titles in the IQ Series:

- *Mixed Martial Arts (Volumes I & II)*
- *New York Yankees*
- *Atlanta Braves*
- *Cincinnati Reds*
- *Boston Red Sox (Volumes (I & II)*
- *Milwaukee Brewers*
- *St. Louis Cardinals (Volumes I & II)*
- *Boston Celtics (Volumes I & II)*
- *University of Florida Gators Football*
- *University of Georgia Bulldogs Football*
- *University of Oklahoma Sooners Football*
- *University of Texas Longhorns Football*
- *West Point Football*
- *Texas A&M Aggies Football*
- *New England Patriots*
- *Buffalo Bills*

For information about special discounts for bulk purchases, please email:

black.mesa.publishing@gmail.com

Black Mesa

www.blackmesabooks.com

*The following is an excerpt from*

# San Francisco Giants: An Interactive Guide to the World of Sports

## Tucker Elliot & Zac Robinson

*Available from Black Mesa Publishing*

"This buried a lot of bones – '62, '89, 2002. This group deserved it, faithful from the beginning. We're proud and humbled by the achievement."

— *General Manager Brian Sabean*

## *Epilogue*

## 2010 World Champions

ON NOVEMBER 1, 2010, the San Francisco Giants won the World Series for the first time since 1954—making it the first title during the San Francisco era of franchise history.

MLB began divisional play in 1969 so it could expand the postseason. The last season the Giants won a pennant pre-divisional play was in 1962, when the club lost a hard-fought seven-game World Series to the New York Yankees. The first season the Giants made the playoffs during this new era of divisional play was 1971, but that club lost the best-of-five National League Championship Series in four games to the Pittsburgh Pirates. It was 1987 before the Giants made a return trip to the postseason and 1989 before the Giants made it back to the World Series—both seasons ended with disappointing losses.

There was more heartbreak in 1997 and 1999, and of course 2002—and again in 2003.

The 1969 Chicago Cubs wasted no time becoming the first team in baseball's expanded postseason era to blow a golden opportunity. The 1969 Cubs spent 156 days in first place in the N.L. East but failed to make the postseason ... despite holding a nine-game lead over the New York Mets on August 16. The Cubs lost eight straight games in early September, won only eight games that entire month, and could do nothing but watch as a nine-game lead turned into a nine-game deficit.

After the 1969 Cubs' epic fail, no team in baseball failed to make the postseason after spending at least 147 or more days in first place until the 2007 New York Mets (159 days in first).

And then it happened again in 2008, to the Arizona Diamondbacks (158 days in first) ... and then again in 2009, to the Detroit Tigers (165 days in first) ... and then, finally, in 2010, a major league team collapsed after leading its division for 147 days during the regular season for the fourth consecutive season, after nearly forty seasons in which it didn't happen a single time.

It was, of course, the San Diego Padres.

On August 25, the Giants trailed the Padres by 6.5 games.

On August 26, the Padres lost the first of ten consecutive games.

On September 25, the Padres fell out of first place for good.

On October 3, the Padres had a chance to conclude the regular season with a sweep at AT&T Park—which would have given the clubs identical records. The Giants prevailed, however, claiming the division after spending just 38 days in first all season.

And with that victory on the final day of the regular season, the 2010 Giants began an unlikely run that culminated with postseason glory. Here's a look back at how they did it, by the numbers.

*2010 Schedule*

*92* First rule, they all count: the Giants won (92) regular season games—and it took every one of them to reach the postseason.

*97* The Giants scored (97) runs during 19 extra-inning games in the regular season. The club was 11-8 when giving fans some free baseball—and it took every one of those 11 extra-inning victories to reach the postseason.

*189* The Giants scored (189) runs during 52 regular season games that were decided by a single run: *52 one-run games.* The club won 28, lost 24—but you got it, it took all 28 of those one-run victories to reach the postseason.

*224* It's true that one-run games are exciting, but blowouts can be fun, too—and the Giants scored (224) runs during 35 regular season games decided by five or more runs, otherwise known as blowouts. San Francisco won 22 of those blowouts and lost only 13.

*467* In fact, when you break down the "splits" from 2010 the only subpar performance was interleague play—the Giants posted a (.467) winning percentage against the American League, winning seven games, but losing eight.

*568* That first rule though, *they all count*: and when it was done, the Giants overall (.568) winning percentage was enough for a division title. The club was 92-70 overall, 49-32 at home, 43-38 on the road, and posted a .500 or better winning percentage in April, May, July, and September. The club's best months were July and September: 20-8 and 18-8. Worst month was August: 13-15. The Giants favorite opponent was the Arizona Diamondbacks: 13-5. Least favorite, no big surprise—the San Diego Padres: only 6-12. But hey, that sixth win against the Padres ... it was *huge*.

*2010 Pitching Stats*

*4* Matt Cain led the pitching staff with (4) complete games— including a team best two shutouts. And here's a telling stat ... Cain led the club with 223-plus innings of work, but he *faced* fewer batters than did Tim Lincecum, who was second on the team with 212-plus innings of work.

*13* Three members of the staff won (13) or more games: Matt Cain, Tim Lincecum, and Jonathan Sanchez.

*16* The Freak led the club with (16) victories. Tim Lincecum was 16-10 and his 231 strikeouts gave him the league's highest total for the third consecutive season.

*33* It takes a lot of things falling into place in order to win a division title, but when your starting rotation boasts four guys who each make exactly (33) starts ... then you're on to something. Matt Cain, Tim Lincecum, Barry Zito, and Jonathan Sanchez all made 33 starts, and they all pitched 190-plus innings.

*48* It helps to have a solid closer to finish things off—and with (48) saves on the season, Brian Wilson is exactly that. Wilson appeared in 70 games, finished 59 of them, posted a 1.81 earned run average, and his 48 saves tied the franchise record set by Rod Beck in 1993.

*178* The team posted a (1.78) earned run average in September—which was the best team effort in baseball for any given month since the Cleveland Indians had a 1.42 ERA in May 1968.

*300* It also helps when you've got a rookie who makes 18 starts and posts a team best (3.00) earned run average. Enter Madison Bumgarner, who did just that.

*336* And it really helps when your pitching staff is the best in the league—and the Giants did in fact lead the league with a team (3.36) earned run average. San Francisco was second in the league with 92 wins, first in ERA, fourth in complete games, fourth in shutouts, first in saves, first in fewest hits allowed, second in fewest runs (including unearned) allowed, third in fewest home runs allowed, and first in strikeouts.

*2010 Offensive Stats*

*18* Pat Burrell hit (18) home runs in only 96 games for the Giants after being released by Tampa Bay earlier in the season. Burrell signed with the Giants on May 29, and his 18 home runs are the most in franchise history for any player who began the season with another team.

*21* Buster Posey had a (21)-game hitting streak in July. He batted .417 for the month with 24 RBI and 43 hits—and he became the first rookie since Ryan Braun in 2007 to win National League Player of the Month honors.

*24* Shortstop Juan Uribe was second on the club with (24) home runs and 85 RBI. Two of his homers and six of his RBI came in the second inning of a 13-0 Giants romp at Wrigley Field on September 23. Uribe became just the second visiting player to homer twice in the same inning against the Cubs.

*100* Aubrey Huff led the team with (100) runs scored. He was also the offensive leader in hits (165), doubles (35), triples (5), home runs (26), and RBI (86).

*121* It was the (121st) season that the Giants and Dodgers battled each other in some form—but the 2010 Giants managed to do something no other team in franchise history had ever done ... it rallied from four runs down to beat the Dodgers on the road not once, but twice in the same season. On July 20, the Dodgers trailed 5-1 but rallied for a 7-5 victory after scoring three ninth-inning runs against Jonathan Broxton. Then on September 4, the Giants trailed 4-0 in the seventh inning, but rallied with four home runs in the final three innings, including a two-run game-winning shot by Juan Uribe off Jonathan Broxton in the ninth. Broxton became just the second Dodgers reliever in 99 years to lose to the Giants three times in one season.

*305* Buster Posey won Rookie of the Year honors after batting (.305) and pounding 43 extra base-hits in just 108 games—good for a .505 slugging percentage. The 2008 first-round draft pick out of FSU was called up in late May and quickly took over as the Giants starting catcher.

*556* Buster Posey was a one-man wrecking crew during the final seven games leading up to the 2010 All-Star break. He batted (.556) and won Bank of America Player of the Week honors for the week of July 5 – 11. Posey was 15 for 27 and also led MLB with 14 RBI—plus, he hit five homers and had a pair of four-hit games.

*2* Buster Posey attempted just (2) steals during the regular season and he was thrown out both times ... but in Game 1 of the Division Series vs. Atlanta, Posey was not only the first rookie catcher in history to bat clean-up in a postseason game, he also had two of the combined seven hits in the game, and he scored the only run of the game *after* stealing his first base of the year to get into scoring position.

*3* Edgar Renteria hit only (3) home runs during 72 regular season games ... but he hit two during five World Series games. The World Series MVP was only 1 for 16 (.063) vs. Philadelphia during the League Championship Series ... but he was 7 for 17 (.412) vs. Texas during the World Series. Renteria's second homer of the series came in the seventh inning of the Giants title-clinching Game 5 win vs. Texas. It proved to be the game-winner, which makes Renteria the first player in MLB history to pick up the game-winning RBI in the seventh inning or later of the title-clinching game of the World Series ... *twice*. He also did it for the 1997 Florida Marlins.

*4* Buster Posey picked up (4) hits during Game 4 of the National League Championship Series vs. Philly, making him only the second rookie catcher in MLB history to collect four hits in a single postseason game. Joe Garagiola did it for the Cardinals in 1946.

*8* Cody Ross was the Giants (#8) hitter during Game 1 of the National League Championship Series vs. Philly. No worries ... all he did was go yard off Roy Halladay ... *twice*. Halladay had given up only two home runs all season to players batting eighth or ninth in the lineup.

*10* And speaking of Cody Ross ... the late-season acquisition drove in (10) runs during the 2010 playoffs, including three vs. Atlanta and five vs. Philly to help the Giants clinch the pennant. In fact, when Ross broke a scoreless tie with a two-run fourth inning single vs. Philly during Game 3 of the NLCS, it was his fourth game-winning RBI of the postseason ... *in only seven games!* That's the fastest any player in history has accumulated four game-winning hits in the postseason.

*14* Tim Lincecum tied a MLB record with (14) strikeouts in his postseason debut. He led the Giants to a 1-0 victory vs. Atlanta during Game 1 of the Division Series with a complete game two-hitter. Lincecum allowed only three base runners—which made him just the second player in MLB history to pitch a complete game shutout in the postseason while striking out at least 14 batters and allowing no more than three base runners. Roger Clemens did it for the Yankees vs. the Mariners in 2000.

*18* Brian Wilson faced (18) batters vs. Philly in the National League Championship Series. Only four of those batters reached base—two hits and two walks—but none of them scored. Wilson earned three saves and a win vs. Philly, making him just the fourth pitcher in MLB history to win or save four games in a series.

*22* The ability to win tight ballgames paid off big time for the Giants during the Division Series vs. the Braves—during the final (22) innings of that series, the biggest lead for either team was ... *one run.* All four of the games in that series were decided by a single run, which made it just the second series in MLB history to open with four consecutive one-run games.

*30* Freddy Sanchez had only (30) extra-base hits during the 2010 regular season for the Giants—but during Game 1 of the World Series vs. Texas, he banged out three doubles vs. Cliff Lee, who had given up only three extra-base hits total during his previous three postseason starts. The Giants rolled to a surprising 11-7 victory—not surprising because the Giants won, but because the pitching matchup was Lincecum vs. Lee and the teams combined for 18 runs.

*85* Matt Cain faced (85) batters during the 2010 postseason ... *and he didn't allow a single earned run.* He made three starts, pitched 21.1 innings, and gave up one unearned run vs. Atlanta, but that was it. He gave up just 13 hits, eight walks, and struck out 13. Cain became the first pitcher in two decades to not allow a single earned run in his first two career postseason starts—and he joined a very elite group when he didn't give up any earned runs in his third start: in MLB history only Christy Mathewson (1905), Waite Hoyt (1921), and Jon Matlack (1973) began their postseason careers with three consecutive starts without allowing an earned run.

*218* Rookie Madison Bumgarner posted a cool (2.18) earned run average during three starts and four total appearances in the 2010 postseason. He was also the winning pitcher in the Division Series clincher at Turner Field. It was the first time since 1981 that a rookie starting pitcher clinched a postseason series on the road. Two guys did it in 1981: Fernando Valenzuela for the Dodgers and Giants pitching coach Dave Righetti, who did it for the Yankees.

*276* The Texas Rangers were the best hitting team in MLB with a (.276) average during the 2010 regular season. The Giants pitching staff held the Rangers to a paltry .190 average during the World Series, while becoming the first team in 30 years to win three World Series games while surrendering one run or less. The Giants staff even held the Rangers scoreless for 18 consecutive innings from Game 3 through the seventh inning of Game 5.

*419* The distance in feet (419) of Buster Posey's home run during Game 4 of the World Series. The bomb capped the Giants scoring, sealing a 4-0 victory and a commanding 3-1 lead in the series. Posey became just the fourth rookie catcher to homer in the World Series. Also in Game 4, Posey and Madison Bumgarner became the first all-rookie battery to start a World Series game since 1947—and Bumgarner tossed eight scoreless innings, becoming the first rookie starter to not allow an earned run in a World Series game since 1987, the first to do so while picking up a victory since 1969, and the first to do so while pitching at least eight innings since 1948.

*The following is an excerpt from*

# St. Louis Cardinals IQ: The Ultimate Test of True Fandom

---

## Larry Underwood

## 2011 Edition (Volume II)

*Available from Black Mesa Publishing*

# First

ST. LOUIS WAS one of the six original members of the American Association, which existed as a major league from 1882 through 1891. They were also the class of this new league, winning four consecutive pennants (1885-1888); they also finished second on three different occasions (1883, 1889, and 1891), before entering a long period of mediocrity (at best) which wouldn't end until the team won its first National League pennant in 1926. Capping off that great season, the Cardinals beat the heavily favored New York Yankees in the World Series. This first inning will test your knowledge of St. Louis Cardinals history from 1882 through 1925. We're going to start off with some ancient history which will test even the most diehard Cardinals historians. Good luck!

### TOP OF THE FIRST

QUESTION 1: Who was the original owner of the Cardinals?
    a) Charlie Comiskey
    b) Chris Von der Ahe
    c) Andrew Van Slyke
    d) Zeke Bonura

QUESTION 2: Name the field manager who led the Cardinals to four consecutive American Association pennants during the 1880s.
    a) Ned Cuthbert
    b) Ted Sullivan
    c) Jimmy Williams
    d) Charlie Comiskey

QUESTION 3: Name the player who posted the highest batting average for the Cardinals during the 1880s.

a) Arlie Latham
b) Tip O'Neill
c) Hugh Nicol
d) Bill Gleason

**QUESTION 4:** Name the player who led the Cardinals with 829 runs scored during the 1880s.
a) Arlie Latham
b) Bill Gleason
c) Tip O'Neill
d) Yank Robinson

**QUESTION 5:** What pitcher recorded the most wins for the Cardinals during the 1880s?
a) Silver King
b) Jumbo McGinnis
c) Bob Caruthers
d) Dave Fouts

**QUESTION 6:** How many wins did the pitching team leader collect during the 1880s?
a) 94
b) 104
c) 114
d) 217

**QUESTION 7:** What team did the Cardinals defeat in the 1886 World Series, to become World Champions?
a) Cleveland Spiders
b) Chicago White Stockings
c) Boston Red Stockings
d) New York Highlanders

**QUESTION 8:** How many runs did the Cardinals score during the 1887 season?
a) 1,031
b) 1,131

c)  1,213
d)  1,311

**QUESTION 9:** After winning four consecutive pennants, the Cardinals finished second to what team in 1889?
a)  Chicago Cubs
b)  Brooklyn Dodgers
c)  New York Giants
d)  Boston Braves

**QUESTION 10:** In 1899, what two brothers formed the new ownership for the Cardinals?
a)  Frank and Stewart Robinson
b)  Stanley and Fred Livingston
c)  Stanley and Frank Robison
d)  Frank and Brooks Robinson

## TOP OF THE FIRST ANSWER KEY

\_\_ **QUESTION 1:** B
\_\_ **QUESTION 2:** D
\_\_ **QUESTION 3:** B
\_\_ **QUESTION 4:** A
\_\_ **QUESTION 5:** D
\_\_ **QUESTION 6:** C
\_\_ **QUESTION 7:** B
\_\_ **QUESTION 8:** B
\_\_ **QUESTION 9:** B
\_\_ **QUESTION 10:** C

**KEEP A RUNNING TALLY OF YOUR CORRECT ANSWERS!**

Number correct:       \_\_ / 10

Overall correct:       \_\_ / 10

QUESTION 11: How many times did the Cardinals finish in last place during the first decade of the 2oth century?
- a) 3
- b) 2
- c) 4
- d) 5

QUESTION 12: Owning the worst team in the National League apparently took its toll on the Robison brothers; Frank died suddenly, in 1908, and three years later, Stanley suffered an untimely death, as well. Who took over the team upon Stanley's demise?
- a) Margaret Chase Smith
- b) Janis Robison Joplin
- c) Helene Curtis Robison
- d) Helene Robison Britton

QUESTION 13: Before the 1917 season, ownership once again transferred to someone else. Who was the new lucky owner?
- a) James Jones
- b) Edward Jones
- c) Thomas Jones
- d) Jonas Edwards

QUESTION 14: Who was hired in 1917, to help run the team's front office?
- a) Roger Bresnahan
- b) Miller Huggins
- c) Mike Gonzalez
- d) Branch Rickey

QUESTION 15: What minor league player and future Hall of Fame member did the Cardinals purchase in 1915?

a) Jim Bottomley
b) Rogers Hornsby
c) Miller Huggins
d) Grover Alexander

QUESTION 16: By 1920, the Cardinals had yet another owner, who also took over the presidency of the club. Who was this person?
a) Jack Stewart
b) Dick Robson
c) Sam Breadon
d) Mark Harnden

QUESTION 17: Name the recent high school graduate the Cardinals signed in 1923 who would become one of the team's great outfielders during his career.
a) Taylor Douthit
b) Chick Hafey
c) Jack Smith
d) Ray Blades

QUESTION 18: What was Rogers Hornsby's batting average in 1924?
a) .412
b) .420
c) .424
d) .418

QUESTION 19: In 1925, what Cardinals player tied a club record for most extra base hits in a game (four), with two home runs and two doubles?
a) Rogers Hornsby
b) Jim Bottomley
c) Ray Blades
d) Les Bell

**QUESTION 20:** Who replaced Branch Rickey as field manager of the Cardinals during the 1925 season?
   a)  Frank Frisch
   b)  Heinie Mueller
   c)  Rogers Hornsby
   d)  Bob O'Farrell

## BOTTOM OF THE FIRST ANSWER KEY

___ **QUESTION 11:** A
___ **QUESTION 12:** D
___ **QUESTION 13:** A
___ **QUESTION 14:** D
___ **QUESTION 15:** B
___ **QUESTION 16:** C
___ **QUESTION 17:** B
___ **QUESTION 18:** C
___ **QUESTION 19:** D
___ **QUESTION 20:** C

**KEEP A RUNNING TALLY OF YOUR CORRECT ANSWERS!**

Number correct:          ___ / 10

Overall correct:          ___ / 20

www.blackmesabooks.com

www.ingramcontent.com/pod-product-compliance
Lightning Source LLC
Chambersburg PA
CBHW060505030426
42337CB00015B/1747